I dedicate this book to my brother Ken,
the first person with whom
I formally explored the topic of play.

"The city streets will be filled
with boys and girls playing there."

—Zechariah 8:5

Contents

● ● ● ● ● ● ● ●

Part III—Adding Your Own Games   255

Game Finder

● ● ● ● ● ● ●

The game finder is an alphabetical listing of all the games in this book followed by the requirements for the game. If you forget where the game is, just look it up by its name and you can quickly retrieve it by its page number. The four columns that follow the page number can also be used to select a game. If you are looking for games by the number of participants, by activity level, by grade level, and by playing area, or any combination of the above, these columns help you find the games you are looking for.

Game	Page No.	Number of Participants	Activity Level	Grade Level	Playing Area
1800's Baseball	153	2 teams 10 per team	Medium	6+	Baseball diamond
1-Down Football	177	2 teams 5-7 per team	Medium	6+	Football field
3-A-Side Hockey	187	2 teams 6+ per team	High	4+	Gym or paved area
3-on-3 Basketball	161	3-5 per team	High	4+	Half of a basketball court
3-Pitch Baseball	139	2 teams 10 per team	Medium	6+	Baseball diamond
3-Pitch Snow Baseball	253	2 teams 10 per team	Medium	6+	Baseball diamond
3 Point Shooting	128	Any number	Low	8+	Basketball court
4 Way Tug-of-War	101	4 teams 4+ per team	High	4+	Anywhere

(continued)

Game	Page No.	Number of Participants	Activity Level	Grade Level	Playing Area
A Quarter Among Friends	43	3+ teams 15-60 per team	Low	4+	Anywhere
ABS Rollerball	63	3+ teams	Medium	8+	Anywhere
Add-3 Volleyball	217	2 teams 9 per team	Medium	6+	Volleyball court
Architects	90	5-10 per team	Low	8+	Anywhere
Backside Tug-of-War	102	2 per contest	High	8+	Anywhere
Balloon Dribble Race	88	4-6 per team	Medium	1+	Gym
Balloon Kick	136	Any number	Low	4+	Anywhere
Balloon Stomp	55	2 teams 5-10 per team	Medium	4+	Gym
Balloon Train Race	89	5-25 per team	Low	1+	Anywhere
Balloons Away	54	5+ per game	Medium	1+	Any defined area
Bank Deposit	31	2 per game	Low	4+	Long table or smooth floor
Bank Robber	32	2 per game	Low	4+	Long table or smooth floor
Bases Loaded	150	2 teams 10 per team	Medium	6+	Baseball diamond
Beanbag Golf	59	1 team per hole 1-4 per team	Medium	8+	Outdoor field
Beanbag Pick Up	96	4+ per team	High	8+	Anywhere
Beat the Ball Home	147	2 teams 10 per team	Medium	4+	Baseball diamond
Best Ball	59	1 team per hole 1-4 per team	Medium	8+	Outdoor field
Bladder Broomball	191	2 teams 6+ per team	High	6+	Ice hockey rink
Bladder Kickball	145	2 teams 10 per team	Medium	4+	Baseball diamond

Game	Page No.	Number of Participants	Activity Level	Grade Level	Playing Area
Blind Puzzle	6	3-7 per team	Low	4+	Flat surface
Blind Soccer	202	2 teams 6 per team	High	4+	Gym
Blind Volleyball	221	2 teams 6 per team	Medium	6+	Volleyball court
Block-Head Relay	79	4-8 per team	Medium	4+	Anywhere
Boor's Ultimate Medical Dodgeball	60	2 teams 5-12 per team	Medium	8+	Basketball court
Boot Hockey	183	2 teams 6-15 per team	High	6+	Gym
Bouncers	164	2-30 people	Medium	4+	Half a basketball court
Broomball	190	2 teams 6+ per team	High	6+	Ice hockey rink
Capped Serves Volleyball	218	2 teams 6 per team	Medium	6+	Volleyball court
Car Trouble	75	4-5 per team	High	4-8	Anywhere
Catch the Chicken	116	4 per team	Low	4+	Anywhere
Catch-and-Pull Tug-of-War	103	2 per contest	High	4+	Anywhere
Caterpillar Race	82	5-12 per team	Medium	4+	Gym or other hard surface
Chariot Races	74	4-6 teams 5-8 per team	High	4+	Large area with hard, flat floor
Chest Wrestling	113	2 per contest	Medium	8+	Anywhere
Chicken Toss	115	2 per team	Low	4+	Anywhere
Co-Ed Basketball	160	2 teams 5-12 per team	High	4+	Basketball court
Co-Ed Volleyball	218	2 teams 3 males per team 3 females per team	Medium	6+	Volleyball court

(continued)

Game	Page No.	Number of Participants	Activity Level	Grade Level	Playing Area
Coiled Rollerball	64	3+ per team	Medium	8+	Anywhere
Coin Golf	41	2-4 per game	Low	4+	Large table or smooth floor
Crabs Away	67	2 teams 8-25 per team	Medium	4+	Anywhere
Crazy Carpet Relay	81	4-5 per team	High	4+	Gym or other hard surface
Crazy Foul Shots	126	Any number	Low	4+	Basketball court
Cross-Out Baseball	148	2 teams 10 per team	Medium	6+	Baseball diamond
Crotchety Pipe Walk	45	5-8 per pipe	Medium	8+	Large flat area
Curling Funspiel	243	2 teams 4 per team	Low	8+	Curling rink
Dime Soccer	38	2 per game	Low	4+	Large table
Dog Sled Race	245	3-5 teams 3 per team	High	8+	Snow-covered area
Double Dutch	132	3-4 per team	High	1+	Anywhere
Double Enormous Volleyball	223	2 teams 8-16 per team	High	8+	Volleyball court
Double Knee Boxing	109	2 per contest	High	4+	Anywhere
Enormous Volleyball	222	2 teams 8-16 per team	Medium	8+	Volleyball court
Everyone Hits	141	2 teams 10 per team	Medium	6+	Baseball diamond
Fishing Forecast	17	Any number	None	6+	Table
Flag Football	167	2 teams 5-7 per team	Medium	6+	Football field
Flip-in-a-Cup	28	2-5 per group	Low	4+	Large table or smooth floor
Floor Ball Hockey	185	2 teams 6+ per team	High	4+	Gym or paved area

Game	Page No.	Number of Participants	Activity Level	Grade Level	Playing Area
Folly Ball	220	2 teams 6 per team	Medium	6+	Volleyball court
Foot Hockey	187	2 teams 6+ per team	High	4+	Gym or paved area
Foul-Points Basketball	159	2 teams 5-12 per team	High	4+	Basketball court
Four-Court Volleyball	225	4 teams 6 per team	Medium	6+	Volleyball court
Four-Goal Soccer	204	4 teams 5-7 per team	High	4+	Gym
Frisbee Baseball	151	2 teams 10 per team	Medium	4+	Baseball diamond
Frisbee Football	170	2 teams 5-7 per team	Medium	6+	Football field
Frisbee Golf	58	1 team per hole 1-4 per team	Medium	8+	Outdoor field
Frisbee Soccer	196	2 teams 11+ per team	High	4+	Soccer field
Frozen Snowballs	239	2 teams 10+ per team	Medium	4+	Basketball court
Going Nuts	53	5-8 per team	Low	4+	Anywhere
Group Triangle	3	3-30 per group	Low	8+	Anywhere
Hackey Sac Dribble	125	Any number	Medium	8+	Anywhere
Half-Court Basketball	159	2 teams 5-12 per team	High	4+	Basketball court
Hand Baseball	143	2 teams 10 per team	Medium	6+	Baseball diamond
Hat Day Races	122	Any number	Low	4+	Anywhere
Heads Up	32	2-10 per group	Low	4+	Large table or flat surface
Hidden Treasure	34	5-10 per group	Low	4+	Anywhere
Hippo Wrestling	114	2 per contest	Medium	8+	Anywhere

(continued)

Game	Page No.	Number of Participants	Activity Level	Grade Level	Playing Area
Hole-in-One	134	Any number	Low	4+	Carpeted surface
Hoop Escape	66	10-20 per team	Medium	8+	Large, flat open area
Human Hurdle Race	80	4-15 per team	High	4+	Anywhere
Human Obstacle Race	86	5-20 per team	Medium	4+	Anywhere
I Like It	18	Any number	None	6+	Anywhere
I See	20	Any number	None	6+	Table
Ice Maker	10	Any number	Low	4+	Anywhere
Inch Football	170	2 teams 5-7 per team	Medium	6+	Wrestling mat
Inchworm Race	83	5-12 per team	High	4+	Gym or other hard surface
Indianapolis 500	73	4-6 teams 5-8 per team	High	4+	Any large area with a flat, hard floor
Indoor Football	173	2 teams 3-5 per team	Medium	8+	Basketball court
Indoor Hand Soccer	202	2 teams 6 per team	High	4+	Gym
Indoor Ice Hockey	182	2 teams 6-15 per team	High	6+	Gym
Indoor Soccer	200	2 teams 6 per team	High	4+	Gym
Inner Tube Basketball	234	2 teams 5 per team	High	8+	Swimming pool
Inner Tube Water Polo	231	2 teams 3-6 per team	High	6+	Swimming pool
JJ Bowling	64	6 per lane	Low	8+	Bowling alley
Kangaroo Hop	106	2 per contest	Medium	4+	Anywhere
Kick Baseball	144	2 teams 10 per team	Medium	4+	Baseball diamond

Game	Page No.	Number of Participants	Activity Level	Grade Level	Playing Area
King of the Kangaroos	107	Any number	Medium	4+	Anywhere
Knee Boxing	109	2 per contest	High	4+	Anywhere
Limited Contacts	47	5-25 per team	Medium	4+	Anywhere
Longest Handstand	117	Any number	Medium	8+	Any walled area
Longest Hula Hoop	119	Any number	High	4+	Anywhere
Longest Spit	120	Any number	Low	4+	Grassy area
Lung Capacity	130	Any number	Low	4+	Anywhere
Mass Outdoor Soccer	198	2 teams 30-75 per team	High	4+	Large field
Matchstick Pull	252	Any number	Low	8+	Anywhere
Money In the Bank	27	2-15 per table	Low	4+	Large table or floor
Monster Basketball	165	2 teams 5-10 per team	High	8+	Basketball court
Monsterball Mass Soccer	199	2 teams 30-75 per team	High	4+	Large field
Nickel Baseball	35	2 per game	Low	8+	Large table
No-Goalie Indoor Soccer	203	2 teams 5+ per team	High	4+	Basketball court
No-Hands Rollerball	64	3-10 per team	Medium	8+	Anywhere
Non-Contact Ice Hockey	179	2 teams 6-15 per team	High	6+	Ice hockey rink
Non-Dominant Basketball	159	2 teams 5-12 per team	High	4+	Basketball court
Noodle Basketball	166	2 teams 5-10 per team	High	8+	Basketball court
Noodle Volleyball	227	2 teams 6-9 per team	High	4+	Volleyball court

(continued)

Game	Page No.	Number of Participants	Activity Level	Grade Level	Playing Area
No-Whistle Hockey	182	2 teams 6-15 per team	High	6+	Ice hockey rink
Offensive Soccer	202	2 teams 6 per team	High	4+	Gym
One-Pass Broomball	191	2 teams 6+ per team	High	6+	Ice hockey rink
One-Touch Soccer	196	2 teams 11+ per team	High	4+	Soccer field
Pairing Off	12	Any number	Low	1+	Anywhere
Paper Pass	10	Any number	Medium	4+	Anywhere
Paper Throw	9	Any number	Medium	4+	Anywhere
Partner Broomball	191	2 teams 6+ per team	High	6+	Ice hockey rink
Pass Pass Football	172	2 teams 5-8 per team	High	6+	Football field
Pass Volleyball	219	2 teams 6-8 per team	Medium	4+	Volleyball court
Paul Revere's Tug-of-War	98	4+ per team	High	8+	Anywhere
Penny Basketball	42	2 per table	Low	4+	Large table
Penny Elbows	25	Any number	Low	4+	Anywhere
Penny Football	37	2 per game	Low	8+	Large table
Penny Roll	24	2-5 per table	Low	8+	Large table or smooth floor
Penoccie	30	2 teams 1-4 per team	Low	8+	Large table
Pin-Down Soccer	204	2 teams 5+ per team	High	4+	Basketball court
Ping-Pong Serve	132	Any number	Low	8+	Ping-Pong table
Pinned-Down Team Handball	213	2 teams 6 per team	High	6+	Basketball court

Game	Page No.	Number of Participants	Activity Level	Grade Level	Playing Area
"Pond" Hockey	184	2 teams 4-20 per team	High	6+	Ice rink
Pool Paddle	237	Any number	High	8+	Swimming pool
Pool Push	236	2 per team	Low	6+	Swimming pool
Push-of-War	100	4+ per team	High	8+	Anywhere
Quarter Drop	26	2-5 per group	Low	4+	Floor
Quarter Hockey	40	2 per game	Low	4+	Large table
Quicksand	7	5-10 per team	Low	8+	Indoors
Quick-Sub Hockey	187	2 teams 6+ per team	High	4+	Gym or paved area
Rear Race	77	5-25 per team	Medium	4+	Anywhere
Recreational Basketball	157	2 teams 5-12 per team	High	4+	Basketball court
Recreational Soccer	193	2 teams 11+ per team	High	4+	Soccer field
Recreational Volleyball	215	2 teams 6 per team	Medium	6+	Volleyball court
Refrigerator Relay	85	4-8 per team	Medium	4+	Anywhere
Rope Rush	97	4+ per team	High	8+	Anywhere
Scavenger Hunt	14	2+ teams 3-5 per team	Medium	4+	Anywhere
Scooter Baseball	154	2 teams 10 per team	Medium	4+	Gym
Scooter Basketball	162	2 teams 5-12 per team	High	4+	Basketball court
Scooter Noodle Hockey	188	2 teams 6-8 per team	Medium	4+	Basketball court
Scooter Soccer	206	2 teams 6-8 per team	High	4+	Gym
Seeing-Eye Dog Sled Race	246	3-5 teams 4 per team	High	8+	Snowy area

(continued)

Game	Page No.	Number of Participants	Activity Level	Grade Level	Playing Area
Sinking Island	13	5-20 per team	Low	8+	Anywhere
Skin the Snake	87	5-15 per team	Low	8+	Anywhere
Skip It	131	Any number	High	1+	Anywhere
Slalom Race	91	4-5 per team	High	8+	Small area with hard floors
Slap Jack	110	2 per contest	High	4+	Anywhere
Sled Hockey	182	2 teams 6-15 per team	High	6+	Ice hockey rink
Snow Bowl	242	Any number	Low	4+	Snow covered area
Snow Sculpture Contest	240	Any number of teams 3-5 per team	Low	4+	Snow covered area
Snow Tug-of-War	247	2 teams 4+ per team	High	8+	Snow covered area
Snowball Fight	248	2 teams 10-15 per team	Medium	8+	Snow covered area
Snow-Boiling Contest	251	3 per team	Low	13+	Outside in a fire pit
Soccer Golf	59	1 team per hole 1-4 per team	Medium	8+	Outdoor field
Soccer Volleyball	226	2 teams 2-4 per team	High	10+	Volleyball court
Sock It to 'Em	68	4+ per contest	High	4+	Padded surface
Sock It to Me	4	Any number	Low	8+	Anywhere
Solo Volleyball	218	1 player per team	Medium	6+	Volleyball court
Sore Toe Relay	78	4-6 per team	High	4-8	Anywhere
Speed Baseball	145	2 teams 10 per team	Medium	6+	Baseball diamond
Speed Hockey	182	2 teams 6-15 per team	High	6+	Ice hockey rink
Speedo	129	Any number	High	8+	Anywhere

Game	Page No.	Number of Participants	Activity Level	Grade Level	Playing Area
Squash Serve	127	Any number	Low	8+	Squash court
Squashed Soccer	209	2 teams 2 per team	High	6+	Squash court
Squatter's Rights	105	2 per contest	Medium	4+	Anywhere
Stork Stand	108	2 per contest	Medium	4+	Anywhere
Straight Rollerball	64	3-10 per team	Medium	8+	Anywhere
String Roll	121	4 per contest	Low	8+	Anywhere with a pole
Stuck Up	111	5-10 per team	Low	8+	Anywhere
Swamp Shoes Relay	83	5-8 per team	High	4+	Smooth, hard surface
Swimming Relay	71	4-5 per team	High	4+	Smooth, hard surface
Tape Roll Bowling	123	Any number	Low	4+	Long hallway
Team Backside Tug-of-War	103	Any number	High	8+	Anywhere
Team Hackey Sac Dribble	125	Any number	Medium	8+	Anywhere
Team Handball	211	2 teams 6 per team	High	6+	Basketball court
The Great Escape	46	5-15 per team	Medium	8+	Beach
Thumb Wrestling	112	2 per contest	Low	4+	Anywhere
Tic-Tac-Toe	33	2 per game	Low	4+	Large table or floor
Timed Tug-of-War	96	4+ per team	High	4+	Anywhere
Toboggan Run	249	5 per team	Low	13+	Snowy hill
Touch Football	170	2 teams 5-7 per team	Medium	6+	Football field
Touch Inner Tube Ball	233	2 teams 5-7 per team	High	8+	Swimming pool
Towel Volleyball	223	2 teams 12 per team	Medium	4+	Volleyball court

(continued)

Game	Page No.	Number of Participants	Activity Level	Grade Level	Playing Area
Traditional Tug-of-War	95	4+ per team	High	8+	Anywhere
Triathlon	51	2+ teams 1-4 per team	High	4+	Gym or hallway
Tubers	246	3-5 teams 2 per team	High	8+	Snowy area
Ultimate Football	175	2 teams 5-15 per team	High	6+	Football field
Ultimate Scooter Football	176	2 teams 5-15 per team	High	6+	Indoor area
Underhand Volleyball	218	2 teams 6 per team	Medium	6+	Volleyball court
Up the Creek	96	4+ per team	High	8+	Creek or muddy field
Uphill Rollerball	64	3-10 per team	Medium	8+	Anywhere
Wall Run	118	Any number	High	4+	Walled area
Water Guzzle	135	Any number	Low	4+	Near a water fountain
Wheeling Around	56	5+ players per game	Medium	8+	Gym or large walled area
World's Strongest Person	124	Any number	Low	8+	Anywhere
Yes or No	21	Any number	None	8+	Anywhere
Ying, Yang, You, Back	48	5-25 per group	Low	8+	Anywhere

Preface

●　●　●　●　●　●　●

A midst the tension of being a student—whether that's orientation into a new school, midterm blues, end-of-semester anxiety, or just the tedium of a tough day of classes—game playing can be a wonderful reprieve. Indeed, game playing allows students to be free, to forget about evaluation, and to focus on doing—to just be kids. In the physical education arena, playing games brings students together, fostering camaraderie, joy, and active participation. Unlike the tedium of calisthenics and the pressures to perform in other school subjects, games provide a wonderful opportunity for kids to lose themselves. From an exercise perspective, kids will put a lot more effort into a fun game than they will put into a boring exercise regimen. And, as any physical education teacher knows, physical activity leads to physical fitness, which brings its own exuberance and satisfaction.

Co-Ed Recreational Games is a collection of games that can be used throughout the teaching year. During orientation and the first few weeks of school, when incoming students are most apprehensive, playing games will warm students to the school itself, to their teachers, and to one another. These games can also be used during the rest of the school year, when stress levels are running high or simply when students need some physical activity or a mental diversion from their studies. Providing the opportunity for students to participate in games gives them a much-needed break from the everyday stresses of school.

Whether you are working with elementary, high school, or university students in physical education, intramural, or after-school programs, this book will help you create fun learning experiences for your students. More important, perhaps, these games—in particular, games that require problem solving—will provide you with an opportunity to observe social interactions among kids.

Use these games as an opportunity to affirm different personality styles. For example, certain games will help you identify the leaders and the followers in each class. Mainstream society currently deems leadership the superior quality. As we all know, however, to succeed, a leader needs followers. Therefore, it is worthwhile to talk with your students about participation and cooperation—specifically, how everyone's effort influenced the team's success. Taught in the context of a game, such insight on leadership, and leadership style, will benefit your students throughout their lives.

Whether teachers, coaches, or youth leaders—with a little game experience or a lot—leaders who use this book will find these games easy to understand and apply. Indeed, one of the unique features of this book is the variety of games included, from the novel to the familiar but with a twist. In chapter 9, for example, kids play basketball while seated on scooters or using a rubber chicken as the ball. Such variations not only make traditional games more entertaining, but they also "level the playing field," so to speak, so that all students can participate, feel included, and have fun. Amassed from more than 20 years of teaching and organizing intramural and other physical recreation programs, the games included in this book are those that consistently evoke the most smiles—and often the most sweat—as well as those in which students most readily lose their inhibitions and just play.

To help you use the more than 200 games included in *Co-Ed Recreational Games* a Game Finder has been included at the beginning. This alphabetical list will help you locate games quickly and select those most suited to the needs of your students, including the number in class, their ages, and the facility and equipment available. Once you are familiar with the activities in this book, to create an effective, rewarding physical education program for your students, choose games that foster the skills you want to develop.

To help you navigate the book, chapters are grouped into three parts. Following an introductory chapter, "Organizing the Fun," Part I: Breaking the Ice (chapters 1 through 7) features games, activities, and riddles that help students feel more comfortable; coin games; group games; team and individual contests; races and relays; and tugs-of-war. Part II: Modifying Traditional Games (chapters 8 through 15) features traditional sport games as well as lively variations of those games, not only to "level the playing field" slightly but also to raise enjoyment and interest levels. Winter games are also included in part II, including lots of winter activities students can enjoy indoors or in the snow. Part III: Adding Your Own Games, the final section of the book, contains only one chapter. But it packs a powerful punch. This chapter outlines a simple, step-by-step plan to conceptualize and record new games for all to enjoy in the years to come.

A games book is like a cookbook. The recipes contained make some delicious concoctions, but most cooks adjust the ingredients to suit their individual tastes. Take the games, and their variations, in this book and modify them further, or come up with your own ideas to suit your tastes. Better yet, you can involve your students in this process, challenging them to adapt an existing game or come up with an entirely new game all their own.

By encouraging and fostering the spirit of game playing in your classroom, your students will learn not only to relish play but also to enjoy physical activity and fitness—two pursuits that will benefit them enormously in the years to come. It may also help you incorporate the fun of game playing into your own life, perhaps motivating you to let go and enjoy life. Ah, to be a kid again. Use the games in this book to nurture the kid in you.

Acknowledgments

• • • • • • •

Special thanks go to a lot of people who contributed to making this book possible. The Canadian Intramural Recreation Association-Ontario folks are always dreaming up new games, both physically active games and mind games; I've used some of their riddles in this book. Thanks for the inspiration.

I also want to thank the wonderful college campus recreation directors in Ontario. In particular, the northern Ontario colleges aren't intimidated by a little cold and snowy weather and have designed many activities to do in the winter. I want to thank Patricia Jackson and Tom Mauro at Canadore College and Sault College for their Winterfest suggestions. Susan Tucker, from her isolated Confederation College post in Thunder Bay, provided a lot of ideas about scavenger hunts. The campus recreation staff at George Brown College provided the Indoor Football rules. Michael Vanderboor, from Jarvis Christian School, graciously contributed the strategic Boor's Ultimate Medical Dodgeball. The work of John van Hove, who is wonderfully creative in his high school intramural programming in Burnaby, provided the inspiration for several games in this book. I have also learned a lot from my colleague in games, Al Brown.

Thanks to the Ontario Ministry of Tourism, Culture and Recreation. While working on a related project to promote active living for Ontario college students, several of the game ideas in this book came together.

Thanks also to Redeemer University College, which not only is a great place to work and play, but it also granted me the sabbatical that made writing this book possible.

Thanks to the staff at Human Kinetics for the support they have given me and their encouragement of physical activity around the world. Special thanks to Amy for her confidence in this project and DK for her editorial skill and for teaching me so much about writing.

Thanks to my wife Catherine, and my children Hannah (and Ryan), Judith, Matt, and Charis, for not demanding more of my time as I worked on this book.

Finally, I want to thank God for putting all things together.

Note: A number of the games in this book were adapted from my experience. Some are modifications of games I discovered at conferences, learned about in discussion, or was taught by students. If I have used games without properly crediting the original source, I would be pleased to correct that in future editions of this book. Here, let me simply thank everyone who has ever discussed games, ideas, and helped me experience the joy of play.

May our streets, parks, schools, and homes be filled with the joy of people freely playing games.

Organizing the Fun

● ● ● ● ● ● ●

Game playing allows physical movement and expression. This is especially important in today's computer-oriented society, in which sedentary interests such as TV and video games are the norm for most kids. Playing games also creates an opportunity to improve creativity, problem-solving skills, and sportsmanship, as well as an opportunity for challenge, social interaction, group solidarity, and fun.

Although the games themselves provide the vehicle to develop these skills, the keys to unlocking them—that is, creating the opportunity—are held by teachers, coaches, and other leaders. Make the most of your game instruction by using the following tips.

- As a leader, be enthusiastic. Your enthusiasm will create excitement in students.
- Have fun and celebrate students' successes.
- Quiet students between games to get their attention and make sure everyone understands the rules.
- Reinforce good sportsmanship with shouts of encouragement during the game and boisterous praise afterward.
- Maximize participation by minimizing the number of students sitting on the sidelines during games.
- Don't be afraid to modify games to suit students' needs or available time, equipment, and facilities.

◉ Always be on the lookout for safety hazards and try to minimize the potential for injury.

◉ Execute line changes quickly so that players can get right back in the game.

The following sections explain the components of effective game teaching. While not exhaustive in the art of teaching games, these topics are important to ensure that kids, young and old, learn to play games in a safe environment that fosters cooperation, responsibility, kindness, and fair play.

HOW TO TEACH THE GAMES

Kids can get antsy in any classroom, but in a gym, with the prospect of a fun game awaiting them, students may have an especially hard time sitting still. You will want to get the game started as quickly as possible yet offer enough instruction so that all students can participate. At the beginning of each class, briefly describe the game and do a quick demonstration. You might even practice a round or two with a few students. Then ask if there are any questions.

Note: Before describing a game, you should have already adapted it to suit your needs, enhance or illustrate your current teaching topic, ensure safe participation, and accommodate the needs of special students. Once the game gets rolling though, you may find it necessary to modify certain rules or add further variations.

SAFETY

Many of the games in this book will be new to many kids. In learning the rules of play—not to mention getting caught up in the excitement of the game—students may forget about safety. As a leader, it will be your responsibility to slow them down and ensure students' safety. The following are several suggestions for maximizing safe play.

◉ Before you set up, check the playing area for potential hazards (potholes, broken glass, stones, puddles, and so on).

⊙ Pad any stationary equipment, such as volleyball or badminton net poles, in case students run into it during play.

⊙ If the game involves the risk of students getting hit by a ball, as in Boor's Ultimate Medical Dodgeball (page 60) or Four-Goal Soccer (page 204), use soft balls. Gator skin and foam balls are good alternatives. Likewise, the bladder of an old ball, such as a soccer ball, volleyball, or basketball, is soft and will not hurt when it makes contact with the body, even when kicked from close by. Ball bladders also move erratically, which "levels the playing field" and raises enjoyment for all.

⊙ Never use walls as start/finish lines or boundaries. Instead, use or draw a line far enough away from the wall so that students will not run into it as they race to the finish or to get the ball (or Frisbee, or puck, or balloon, and so on).

⊙ Post an emergency plan and use it. You may want to hold practice drills once a month to remind younger students of correct emergency procedure.

⊙ Make sure that someone qualified in CPR and first aid is readily available for emergencies.

⊙ Require students to wear proper safety equipment, such as eye protection in squash and racquetball, helmets with face masks for hockey, and shin pads in soccer.

⊙ Encourage safe competition. If some students are goofing around or playing a game in an unsafe manner, stop play immediately. Discuss potential hazards and remind them of the safety requirements. Then continue the game, enforcing safety. If students ignore your warnings and continue to roughhouse, eject them from the game.

⊙ Create an atmosphere of voluntary participation. Warn students of the inherent risks of each game and give them an "out" if they need it. Students should feel free to stop participating if they feel unsafe.

TEAM SELECTION

Publicly selecting teams can lead to ridicule and humiliation for the last players chosen. Fortunately, team selection can be done quickly and with laughter. Following are several ways to work some fun into team selection.

1. Line students up, then do the following:

   ⊙ Divide the line into as many segments as the number of teams you need. This is particularly helpful if you want to keep friends together.

   ⊙ Number them off: "1, 2, 3, 4," and so on. This is a useful approach if you want students to mingle and meet each other, since students will usually cluster with friends.

Note: If you want to have an equal number of boys and girls on each team, have the boys stand in one line and the girls in another, each line facing the other. Then separate the lines into teams using either method.

2. Have students, without talking, line up in alphabetical order of their first names, the second letter of their first names, their last names, and so on. (You can also have them line up in order of their birthdays.) Count students off according to how many teams you want. For example, if you want 5 teams, count off up to 5: "1, 2, 3, 4, 5, 1, 2, 3," and so on.

3. Pair students off, then do the following:

   ⊙ The student with the earliest birthday goes on one team while the other student goes on the other.

   ⊙ Have one student sit and the other remain standing. Sitters go on one team and standers go on the other.

4. Distribute objects and group students according to similarities. For example, if you handed out playing cards, players would team up according to suit (spades and clubs on one team, hearts and diamonds on the other). You could also use animal cards. At the signal, students make the sound of the animal on their cards and go around the gym to find their similar-sounding teammates. (If you want to make this really challenging, try using cards with different types of birds on them.)

5. Group students by identifying characteristics:
   ◉ Shirt color
   ◉ Date of birth (team up by season)
   ◉ Birth order in the family
   ◉ Number of letters in their names

6. Have students write their names on a card (or Popsicle stick, or piece of paper, and so on). Then draw names to assign teams.

7. Use games to separate students into teams.
   ◉ Rock, paper, scissors. Pair students off and have them play a round—winners go on one team and losers go on the other. If you need 4 teams, play another round within the 2 teams.
   ◉ Musical hoops. Scatter hula hoops around the gym and play some music. Stop the music and call out the number of students you want in each hoop. Only that many students can stand in a hoop. If a hoop is full, "extra" students have to find another hoop to stand in. Use as many hoops as the number of teams you want (or have twice as many and join 2 groups). For example, if you had 24 students and needed 4 teams, you would put out 4 hoops and call out "six." If friends congregate in the same hoop and exclude other students from getting into "their" hoop, do the exercise again, this time using 8 hoops and calling out "three." Combine students from 2 different hoops to get teams of 6 players.

TRANSITIONING BETWEEN GAMES

The right mix of games goes a long way toward keeping students focused and interested in the class. But efficient transitioning from one game to the next can also enhance the overall experience of a physical education class, not only for students but for teachers as well. Efficient transitioning simply involves moving quickly and easily from one activity to the next. This is accomplished by planning ahead and combining games that require similar equipment or concepts. For example, Quicksand (see page 7) uses a tarp.

When that game is over, you (or students) will need to fold up the tarp. If you follow that game with a game such as Sinking Island (see page 13), however, the tarp is folded as part of the game. Another example of efficient transitioning might be Balloons Away (see page 54), which requires students to blow up balloons, followed by Balloon Stomp (see page 55), which requires students to pop balloons.

It also helps students if a game builds on the concepts of a previous game. For example, Bouncers (see page 164) teaches students to dribble, while Co-Ed Basketball (see page 160) assumes students can dribble. Thus, if your students do not know how to dribble, it would be best to start the class with Bouncers and then proceed to Co-Ed Basketball.

GAME SEQUENCE

If you have time for more than one game, choose the order carefully. The following are some tips for effective game sequencing.

- If you want to use a game that involves close physical contact, save it for later—later during the class or, if you're at the beginning of a school term, later in the term. Start with a game that allows students to become comfortable bumping into each other.

- Let students catch their breath by interspersing low- and medium-activity games with high-activity games. Likewise, determine ahead of time the level of excitement you want students to leave your class with. For example, if you want them to leave feeling excited, maybe at the end of the day, conclude your class with a high-activity game. If they are going to another class, however, such as mathematics or another subject that requires concentration, end the class with a low-activity game.

- Start off with a simple game that students can understand quickly and save the more complicated games for a little later in the class.

FAIR PLAY

"That's not fair! He got to play longer than I did!" It's a call that echoes in gymnasiums across the country. No matter what you do, some students will always think they got gypped out of something. Nevertheless, it is your job to make sure that the game is as fair as possible. In recreational games, inequity typically takes two forms: unequal playing time and gender discrimination.

When it comes to playing time, the best way to prevent player protests and distressed cries of unfairness is to use consistent line changes and player substitutions. If players trade places every 2 minutes, for example, every student will get to play. Even if some students get to play an extra 2 minutes, every player will be pretty much even in terms of class playing time. Of course, time increments will vary according to the game being played. In basketball, football, hockey, and soccer, among others, 2-minute line changes are fine. In relays and races, however, you'll have to allow enough class time so that every participant can run the course at least once. For other types of activities, such as those in which available equipment limits the number of students who can participate at one time, try to allow enough time for everyone to get an equal number of turns.

The subject of gender discrimination is not so clear-cut. Thus, it is your job to make sure that girls get their fair share of time on the court. Luckily, there are ways to structure teams and rules of play so that girls are not left out.

First and foremost, start by ensuring equal gender distribution on teams. The following table lists even gender makeups for different sizes of teams.

Gender Equity Table

Team Numbers	Girls	Boys	Girls or Boys
3 on 3	1	1	1
4 on 4	2	2	
5 on 5	2	2	1
6 on 6	3	3	

Maintaining this girl-boy ratio, then, means having to change lines equitably as well. In games that involve individual substitution of players, for example, Co-Ed Basketball (page 160) and Co-Ed Volleyball (page 218), substitute a boy with a boy and a girl with a girl.

Note: A common variation to such a team makeup is not counting the goalie. For example, Indoor Soccer (page 200) teams of 5 players and 1 goalie could have either a girl or boy in the net and 3 boys and 2 girls, or 3 girls and 2 boys, on the field. Although not ideal—you could end up with 4 boys and 2 girls, or 4 girls and 2 boys, on the field—this variation may seem fair to students, particularly if one gender is more prominent than the other.

Sometimes gender discrimination is more complicated than having more males than females in the game at one time. Even when the number of girls equals the number of boys on the field, some boys will still try to exclude girls during play. For example, some boys may try to prevent the girls from playing by passing the ball or puck only to other boys. Some boys may "dive" in to catch or get control of a ball when it would otherwise be caught or controlled by a girl.

Talk with your students about gender discrimination. If talking doesn't change their attitudes and behavior, try instituting some or all of the following rules during play.

- The ball (or puck or Frisbee, and so on) must be passed to a girl before a goal can be scored.
- Goal (or basket or point, and so on) scoring must alternate between boys and girls. That is, a girl scores a goal, then a boy, then a girl, and so on. If this order is not followed, the goal does not count.
- Points (or goals or baskets, and so on) scored by girls count double.

In the end, games are meant to be enjoyed. It will be your responsibility as a leader to make sure that happens. Do whatever you can to create an opportunity for students to enjoy the game, enjoy one another, have fun, be physically active, learn something about the world or themselves, and leave feeling proud of their accomplishments. Their smiles and enthusiasm on the way out, and at the start of the next class, will let you know how you're doing.

part 1

Breaking the Ice

chapter 1

Ice Breakers and Riddles

GROUP TRIANGLE

Number of Participants	Grade Level	Activity Level	Playing Area
3 to 30	8 and above	Low	Anywhere

Recommended Equipment

- 1 rope, approximately 1 yard (meter), per player
- 1 blindfold per player

Setup

Blindfold students and line them up, side by side, facing the same direction. Divide them into teams and have teammates hold hands. Place each rope in a pile 1 yard (meter) in front of the middle of each line of team members.

How to Play

At the signal, players walk forward, find their rope as a team, and pick it up. With every player touching the rope, each team

tries to make an equilateral triangle within a designated time frame (usually 4 to 5 minutes). The best triangle wins.

Safety Considerations

If students lose contact with the rope, you may need to help them get back to their teams.

Teaching Tips

It can be interesting to observe who takes control and how. After the game, take the opportunity to discuss group leadership and problem solving.

SOCK IT TO ME

Number of Participants	Grade Level	Activity Level	Playing Area
Any number	8 and above	Low	Anywhere

Recommended Equipment

- 1 sock per player
- 1 piece of paper per player

Setup

Give each player a sock and a piece of paper. Have students write their names on the paper and place it inside the sock. Collect the socks and then give each player a sock with another player's name in it, along with a rules sheet. (Print up enough rules sheets ahead of time.) This game is played outside of class and is usually done over a 3-day period.

How to Play

The basic game involves stealing socks. Players start by looking at the name inside their own socks and then trying to steal that player's sock. For example, Player 1 has the name of Player 2 in his sock. Once he steals Player 2's sock, he looks at the name inside Player 2's sock (Player 3) and then tries to steal her (Player 3's) sock. Once a player's sock has been stolen, that player is out of the game.

Players hand in stolen socks immediately to be counted. When the game is over, the player with the most socks wins.

Rules

- Players must wear their socks at all times during play, stuffed no more than 3 inches (7 centimeters) into a pocket or waistband. (Be sure to ask players to dress appropriately on game days—no dresses or body suits.)
- "Safe zones," territories where players' socks cannot be taken, include the following: classrooms, libraries, dorm rooms, anywhere off campus, and job sites.

Safety Considerations

Caution players to use discretion when stealing socks. For example, it would not be prudent, or fair, to steal the sock of a player who is helping a physically disabled student down the stairs.

Teaching Tips

The game must begin at a designated time on a specific date, so that everyone starts at the same time, and usually lasts 3 to 4 days.

Make yourself available, or designate a few leaders, to smooth out any glitches. An example of a glitch is 2 players getting each other's names. For example, Tom gets Susan's name and Susan gets Tom's name. Once Susan steals Tom's sock, she will have no one else to get (her own name is in Tom's sock). In cases like these, you'll have to arrange an exchange with another player so that Susan can continue stealing more socks.

BLIND PUZZLE

Number of Participants	Grade Level	Activity Level	Playing Area
3 to 7 players per team	4 and above	Low	Any flat surface (preferably out of the wind)

Recommended Equipment

- 1 blindfold per team
- 1 puzzle per team

Setup

Make each puzzle: Use a felt marker to line the outside edge of a piece of construction paper, then cut the paper into 6 or 7 pieces (triangles, rectangles, and squares) and put the pieces into a file folder. To make things fair, cut out similar patterns for each team.

How to Play

Blindfold a player on each team. Only she may touch the puzzle pieces. The rest of the team may instruct the blindfolded player but may not touch any of the pieces or the player constructing the puzzle. The first team that puts the construction paper back into its original form wins the game.

Safety Considerations

Rambunctious students may be tempted to poke or play jokes on the blindfolded player. Put a stop to these temptations at the beginning of the game by warning students that their team will be disqualified if this type of behavior ensues.

Teaching Tips

Clear communication skills and encouraging others are important aspects of leadership, particularly when it seems easiest to do it yourself. Use this game to start a class discussion about leadership.

QUICKSAND

Number of Participants	Grade Level	Activity Level	Playing Area
5 to 10 players per team	8 and above	Low	Best played indoors

Recommended Equipment

- 1 tarp (10 × 12 feet or larger) per team
- Duct tape or felt markers

Setup

Using either felt markers or duct tape, make a grid on each tarp. Duplicate this grid on a separate sheet of paper to make a map, marking a pathway through the "quicksand" with Xs. (Each team referee will need a copy of the map.)

Divide students into teams and instruct each team to appoint a referee. Line team members up, single file, on one side of each tarp with the referee on the opposite side.

How to Play

Players make their way across the tarp, one at a time. As soon as a player stands on a square not marked with an X on the map, the referee says, "Squish," and that player goes to the back of the line. The next player then starts across the tarp. Players move across the tarp until they successfully complete the course or step in quicksand. Once players make it across safely, they sit down on the referee's side of the tarp. The first team to complete the course wins.

Rules

- Pathways must be marked either directly forward or backward, or to the right or left—there are no diagonal moves.
- Players must stay on the path. No one is permitted to jump from one part of the path to another part or to miss any squares.
- Only 1 player may be on the tarp at a time.

Safety Considerations

Players should walk across the path, not run or jump, so that the tarp does not slip or slide beneath them.

Teaching Tips

You may help players out by telling them how many Xs and turns there are in the pathway. Starting with a simpler course (perhaps 11 Xs and 4 corners) might be best to introduce the game.

PAPER THROW

Number of Participants	Grade Level	Activity Level	Playing Area
Any number	4 and above	Medium	Anywhere

Recommended Equipment

⊙ 2 sheets of scrap paper per player

Setup

Hand out 2 sheets of paper to each player and have them crumple each one into a wad.

How to Play

Try the following contests:

1. Experiment with different ways of tossing and catching the wad. For example, players can flick the wad up above their heads, bounce it off their knees, and then catch it. (Try this with both crumpled wads at the same time.)

2. With partners, try different ways of throwing and catching the paper wads. (This can turn into quite a team-juggling display.)

Try either of these with teams of 3 or more players.

3. In long team chains, try passing paper wads along the chain without dropping them. (The more wads being passed at the same time, the faster the pace of the game.)

4. Divide the class into 2 teams and position them in lines opposite each other (the distance between them should be at least 5 yards [meters]). Play some music and have team members throw the paper wads to the other team until the music stops. The team with the fewest papers on their side wins.

Safety Considerations

To avoid possible eye injuries, do not allow students to throw the paper at others' heads.

Teaching Tips

To help students learn each other's names, try the following variation.

Paper Pass

Divide students into teams of 4 players. Player 1 holds the crumpled wad, passes it to Player 2, and says "[Player 1's name] passes to [Player 2's name]." If players do not know the next player's name, they should ask before passing the paper. Once team members know one another's names, join 2 teams together (to form a team of 8 players) and use 2 wads of paper.

ICE MAKER

Number of Participants	Grade Level	Activity Level	Playing Area
Any number	4 and above	Low	Anywhere

Recommended Equipment

- 1 card (with "nice" written on it) per player
- 1 card (with "ice" written on it) per game

Setup

Explain the rules and distribute "nice" cards to every student except one. Without being detected, give 1 student the "ice" card. (He is the ice maker.) Instruct students not to tell anyone what is written on their cards and to put their cards in their pockets. Students then walk around the designated area.

How to Play

The ice maker freezes the "nice" players by winking at them. When players are frozen, they must stop where they are, silently count to 5, and then scream, indicating that they had been frozen. Players who have been frozen may not reveal the identity of the ice maker, nor may they help other players identify the ice maker.

When a player, who has not yet been frozen, thinks she knows who the ice maker is, she puts up her hands over her head and says, "I accuse the ice maker!" If she is correct, the ice maker screams in agony and the game is over. If the accuser is incorrect, she screams in agony and is then frozen for the count of 5.

The goal of the game is to identify the ice maker before getting frozen. The ice maker's goal is to freeze as many players as possible before getting caught.

Safety Considerations

To prevent trips and potential injuries caution students not to walk around with their eyes closed to avoid getting frozen.

Teaching Tips

To make the game more challenging, designate 2 (or more) ice makers, depending on how many students are playing. In addition to freezing "nice" players, either ice maker may freeze the other.

PAIRING OFF

Number of Participants	Grade Level	Activity Level	Playing Area
Any number	1 and above	Low	Anywhere

Recommended Equipment

⊙ None

Setup

Position students randomly around the playing area. Call out a characteristic that students may have in common. Some examples are:

⊙ First letter of their given name (or last name, or middle name)
⊙ First letter of a parent's first name (designate which parent beforehand)
⊙ Month of birth (or first letter of birth month)
⊙ Favorite color (or number, or animal, or sport, or musical group, and so on)

How to Play

Once the characteristic is called out, students must quickly find someone with whom they share that characteristic. Students who haven't found a partner within 10 seconds gather together to sing a song ("Mary Had a Little Lamb" or other). After the song, call out a different characteristic. Play continues for 7 to 10 rounds.

Safety Considerations

None

Teaching Tips

An activity like this helps students feel comfortable with each other by finding out characteristics or favorite things they share. The best part of this activity is, these characteristics are endless. Take some time before class to think of many characteristics your students may share. The more they have in common, the more camaraderie they will develop.

SINKING ISLAND

Number of Participants	Grade Level	Activity Level	Playing Area
5 to 20 players per team	8 and above	Low	Anywhere

Recommended Equipment

⊙ 1 tarp per team

Setup

Divide students into teams, then have each team stand on their designated tarp. These tarps are their "islands." Tell students that sharks are circling the islands and no one can get off the island unless excused.

How to Play

A large wave comes along and wipes out half of each island. Students must fold their tarps in half while remaining on their islands. Then another large wave hits. Students fold their tarps in half again. After several waves, it will be almost impossible to fold the tarp and stay on it at the same time. (At this point, you can eliminate the sharks and allow students to get off their islands once the waves hit, each time folding their tarps and then getting back on.)

As waves continue to hit, it will become very difficult for teams to remain on their tarps. When players fall or have to step off the island, their teams are disqualified. The team left standing on the smallest island wins.

Safety Considerations

To prevent injury and/or falls, do not allow students to sit on one another's shoulders.

Teaching Tips

Up to 20 students can typically stand on a square-foot tarp, but larger students may find this difficult.

This is a great game after another activity that involves a tarp—fast and easy cleanup!

SCAVENGER HUNT

Number of Participants	Grade Level	Activity Level	Playing Area
2 or more teams of 3 to 5 players	4 and above	Medium	Anywhere

Recommended Equipment

⊙ 1 list of items per team

Setup

Assign teams or allow students to sign up as a team. Distribute a list of the items to find (each team gets 1 list). Designate judges

(2 to 3 students) and a judging location where teams should return the items at the end of the scavenger hunt. (This location could be part of a celebration at the end of the hunt.)

How to Play

Teams have a certain amount of time (usually 2 to 3 days or class periods) to gather as many items from the list as possible. (A sample list follows.) Each listed item is worth a certain number of points, which are tallied when teams turn in the items at the end of the hunt. (Once the counts are tallied, all items are returned to team members.) The team with the most points wins.

Common Objects
- 20—Paintbrush
- 25—Baseball glove
- 40—Hula hoop
- 50—Canoe paddle
- 50—Rosary or Jewish Yarmulke
- 60—Set of pinochle cards
- 75—Rugby ball
- 75—Pair of bowling shoes

City Objects
- 20—Cross-town bus schedule
- 25—National flag
- 50—Expired ticket to a local sport event
- 60—A pink lawn flamingo
- 75—Business card from a local company (signed by an employee)
- 75—Map of a state/province not adjacent to yours
- 100—Accurate explanation of how the city (or school) got its name
- 125—Official charitable tax receipt

School Objects
- 10—Piece of chalk

- 20—Envelope with school logo
- 30—School brochure
- 30—Piece of paper signed by the janitor
- 35—Scholarship application
- 50—Old yearbook or class picture
- 100—Last year's school parking pass

Clothing

- 20—Purple shoelace
- 20—Bow tie
- 30—Non-digital watch
- 50—Wide, colorful tie
- 100—T-shirt with a picture of a retired politician on it
- 150—Mickey Mouse hat

Money

- 25—Foreign coin
- 50—Foreign bill

Team Photographs

- 75—By the city welcome sign
- 75—With a bus driver
- 100—Playing on playground equipment
- 100—In Halloween costumes
- 150—With a police officer
- 150—With a horse
- 170—At a local tourist attraction
- 250—Boarding a plane

Safety Considerations

None

Teaching Tips

A scavenger hunt is an ideal way for students to have some fun and get to know their school and community. Modify the previous list or use it to generate your own ideas.

FISHING FORECAST

Number of Participants	Grade Level	Activity Level	Playing Area
Any number	6 and above	None	Table

Recommended Equipment

- 3 dice, preferably different colors

Setup

Designate a leader, then tell him the pattern and swear him to secrecy. Position students so that they can see the dice and hear the leader.

How to Play

The number of dots on each dice stands for the number of ice holes, polar bears, and/or hunting parties. Players try to determine the fishing forecast by determining the pattern on the dice. (When there are lots of ice holes open, few polar bears around the ice, and few hunting parties to bother the fish, the fishing forecast is good. When there are few ice holes open, lots of polar bears around the ice, and lots of hunting parties to bother the fish, the fishing forecast is bad.)

The leader throws all 3 dice and then identifies how many ice holes there are, as well as the number of polar bears and hunting parties in the area. When a student thinks she understands the pattern, she must explain the next few throws. If she is correct, swear her to silence and see if anyone else can identify the pattern.

The patterns work as follows:

Pattern #1

- ⊙ 2 = small hunting party
- ⊙ 4 = medium hunting party
- ⊙ 6 = large hunting party

Pattern #2

- ⊙ 1 = 1 ice hole (with no polar bears)
- ⊙ 3 = 1 ice hole with 2 polar bears
- ⊙ 5 = 1 ice hole with 4 polar bears

There are many possible combinations, of course, but here are a few examples:

- ⊙ A roll of 1, 4, 5 equals 2 ice holes with 4 polar bears and a medium hunting party. Not a good time to go fishing.
- ⊙ A roll of 3, 4, 6 equals 1 ice hole with 2 polar bears and a medium and large hunting party. Not a good time to go fishing.
- ⊙ A roll of 1, 1, 1 equals 3 ice holes with no polar bears or hunting parties. An ideal time to go fishing.

Safety Considerations

Warn students not to put dice in their mouths and to toss them gently.

Teaching Tips

This game can be played periodically over several days or weeks until everyone understands it.

I LIKE IT

Number of Participants	Grade Level	Activity Level	Playing Area
Any number	6 and above	None	Anywhere

Recommended Equipment

⊙ None

Setup

Designate a leader. Tell her the pattern and swear her to secrecy.

How to Play

The leader says a few combinations, pairing similar items as instructed by the teacher. Students try to identify the pattern. When a student thinks he has identified the pattern, he suggests a few combinations. If correct, he can help the leader suggest other combinations until other, and eventually all, students understand it.

Combinations go as follows:

⊙ I like geese but dislike ducks.
⊙ I like tennis but dislike squash.
⊙ I like cotton but dislike silk.
⊙ I like moose but dislike bears.

Pattern: I like anything with double letters but dislike anything similar without double letters.

Safety Considerations

None

Teaching Tips

To foster cooperation, divide students into 3 or more teams. One at a time, each team can ask the leader a question to figure out the pattern. The next team should ask a question a few minutes later. Between questions, students can brainstorm to come up with the answer or more questions.

I SEE

Number of Participants	Grade Level	Activity Level	Playing Area
Any number	6 and above	None	Table

Recommended Equipment

○ 8 straws

Setup

Designate a leader and reveal the pattern. Give her the straws and position students around a table so that they can hear and see her.

How to Play

The leader thinks of a number between 1 and 10 and then tosses the straws in a heap on the table. She then, inconspicuously, places a combination of fingers to total that number on the edge of the table. For example, if she was thinking of the number 5, she could put out two fingers on one hand and three fingers on the other. Likewise, she could put out one finger on one hand and four fingers on the other. Players then try to guess the number. They will be looking at the straw combination, but they should be looking at the leader's fingers.

See how long it takes students to figure out the pattern. When a student thinks he knows it, he calls out the number on the next few straw tosses. If he is correct, he should not tell the others how to figure it out. Play continues until everyone understands that they should look at the leader's fingers, not the straws.

Safety Considerations

Instruct leaders to drop the straws gently on the table.

Teaching Tips

Instead of straws, you can use toothpicks, pieces of string, scraps of paper—anything.

YES OR NO

Number of Participants	Grade Level	Activity Level	Playing Area
Any number	8 and above	None	Anywhere

Recommended Equipment

○ None

Setup

Position students in a circle so that everyone can see and hear you.

How to Play

Say the riddle (the following riddles will get you started, but try to come up with your own) and then students try to solve it. Students can get more information by asking yes or no questions, one at a time.

Spilled Milk in the Cabin

Riddle: There is spilled milk in a cabin. Why did the milk get spilled?

Answer: The milk spilled during a plane crash, in the cabin of the plane.

Directions to Town

Riddle: Two friends are walking down a road to get to Smithsville. When they come to a fork in the road, they go to a nearby house to ask for directions. The friends know that two twin brothers live in this house. One brother always tells the truth and the other always lies. Both brothers are very busy, so the friends may ask whoever comes to the door only one question. What should they ask?

Answer: What road would your brother say is the right road to town? (Then they should take the other one.) If the truthful brother answers the door, he will respond with the wrong way to town because that is what his brother would say. If the brother who lies answers the door, he will also respond with the wrong way because he would lie about what his honest brother would say. Either way, the friends would be told the wrong way to town, so they should take the other road.

Operation

Riddle: A father and son are rushed to the hospital. Upon seeing the boy, the doctor says, "I cannot operate on this boy. He's my son." How is this possible?

Answer: The doctor is the boy's mother.

Safety Considerations

None

Teaching Tips

Do not allow the students who quickly solve the riddles to make fun of those who take longer to catch on. If students vary widely in their riddle-solving abilities, it might be a good idea to divide students into 3 or more teams. Teams can then ask yes or no questions, one team at a time, and brainstorm between questions to solve the riddle or come up with more questions.

chapter 2

Coin Challenges

The games in this chapter are described using different coins, but any coin will do. In some games, the smaller the coin, the larger the challenge. In other games, the larger the coin, the larger the challenge. In a game like Tic-Tac-Toe (page 33), for example, in which a player tries to get a coin into a specified area, a smaller coin is easier. In a game such as Penny Football (page 37), a player tries to get a coin to hang over the edge of a table and, thus, a larger coin is easier.

In a game such as Nickel Baseball (page 35), using any coin has pros and cons. Dime bases would be easier to hit off the table than quarter bases because dimes are lighter, but dimes would be more difficult to hit because they are smaller. Feel free to experiment with different coins to make each game interesting and challenging for players. *Note:* if getting the coins back is an issue, use pennies and nickels.

PENNY ROLL

Number of Participants	Grade Level	Activity Level	Playing Area
2 to 5 students per table	4 and above	Low	Large table or smooth floor

Recommended Equipment

- 1 large table per group
- 1 nickel per table
- 1 penny per player

Setup

Place a nickel near one end of a long table. Line up students at the other end of the table.

How to Play

One at a time, players roll a penny down the table, trying to get it to stop close to the nickel. Pennies that roll off the table may be retrieved but may not be rolled again in that round. All pennies are left on the table until the last player has rolled. If the nickel moves during the game, it is returned to its starting position.

The penny closest to the nickel wins 1 point. The first player to score 10 points wins the game. (Players should call out the score after each round so that everyone remembers what the score is.)

Safety Considerations

Do not allow students to run around the table to retrieve their pennies.

Teaching Tips

For faster play, place a nickel half-way down the table, a dime three-quarters of the way down the table, and a quarter at the end of the table. The penny closest to the nickel is worth 1 point, the penny closest to the dime is worth 2 points, and the penny closest to the quarter is worth 3 points. The first player to score 10 points wins.

PENNY ELBOWS

Number of Participants	Grade Level	Activity Level	Playing Area
Any number	4 and above	Low	Anywhere

Recommended Equipment

- ◉ 1 penny per player

Setup

One at a time, have students get into the starting position: right hand, palm down, on the right shoulder. With the left hand, each student places a penny on the right elbow.

How to Play

From the starting position, students drop their right elbows and, with their right hands, try to catch the penny before it hits the floor. A successful catch is worth 1 point. Each student takes 10 turns and then the next student tries. The student with the highest score (out of 10) wins.

Safety Considerations

Make sure that students are far enough away from each other, and far enough from desks, chairs, and other obstacles they might swing their hands into.

Teaching Tips

If catching 1 penny is too easy, make the game more challenging by having students try to catch 2 or more pennies at the same time. Likewise, have students try to simultaneously catch a penny from both elbows.

QUARTER DROP

Number of Participants	Grade Level	Activity Level	Playing Area
2 to 5 players per group	4 and above	Low	Floor

Recommended Equipment

- 1 cup per group
- 4 quarters per player

Setup

Divide students into groups. Place a cup on the floor near each group.

How to Play

One at a time, players hold a quarter in front of them, at eye level, and then drop it into the cup. If they miss or if the quarter bounces out of the cup, the quarter remains on the floor and the next player goes. If the quarter stays in the cup, that player picks up the quarter along with any quarters on the floor. When players are out of quarters, they are out of the game.

Play continues until 1 player has all the quarters. If 2 players are left and neither can score in four tries, then everyone gets their quarters back and is back in the game.

Safety Considerations

Do not let players throw their quarters into the cup.

Teaching Tips

This can also be an individual game. Students drop their quarters into their cups, earning 1 point for every quarter that stays in the cup. The student with the most points out of 20 tries wins.

MONEY IN THE BANK

Number of Participants	Grade Level	Activity Level	Playing Area
2 to 15 players per table	4 and above	Low	Large table or a floor

Recommended Equipment

- Marker or tape
- 3 pennies per player

Setup

Designate the "bank vault" on the table or floor using a marker or tape. The vault should be approximately 1 square yard (meter). Line up students, single file, 2 yards (meters) away from the vault.

How to Play

One at a time, players take turns throwing their pennies into the bank. Player 1 tosses his first penny, trying to get it to stay in the bank. If he misses, the penny stays where it lands and it is Player 2's turn. If she misses, it is Player 3's turn, and so on. When players get their pennies to stay in the bank, they get to pick up their pennies and any pennies thrown before theirs. When players are out of pennies, they are out of the game.

Play continues until 1 player has all the pennies. If 2 players are left and neither can score within four tries, everyone gets all their pennies back and is back in the game.

Safety Considerations

To avoid injuries that might result from being hit with a coin, make sure that players stand behind the thrower during the game.

Teaching Tips

To make the game more challenging, have students toss their pennies from further back. To make the game easier, have them stand closer to the vault.

FLIP-IN-A-CUP

Number of Participants	Grade Level	Activity Level	Playing Area
2 to 5 players per group	4 and above	Low	Large table or smooth floor

Recommended Equipment

- 1 cup per group
- 1 spoon per group
- 3 dimes per player

Setup

Divide students into groups and position each team around a large table (or in clusters on the floor). Place a coffee cup in front of each team. Demonstrate the starting position: balance a spoon between two of your fingers approximately 10 inches (30

centimeters) away from the cup and place a dime in the bowl portion of the spoon.

How to Play

From the starting position, each student takes turns trying to flip a dime into the cup by hitting the handle of the spoon with the other hand. If a player misses, he puts the dime into the cup and then the next player goes. If he gets his dime into the cup, he gets all the dimes. When players are out of dimes, they are out of the game.

Play continues until 1 player has all the dimes. If 2 players are left but neither can score within four tries, everyone gets their dimes back and is back in the game.

Safety Considerations

To prevent sore hands, make sure players hit the end of the spoon, not their fingers.

Teaching Tips

To make the game more challenging, use quarters or nickels.

PENOCCIE

Number of Participants	Grade Level	Activity Level	Playing Area
2 teams of 1 to 4 players	8 and above	Low	Large table

Recommended Equipment

- 1 nickel
- 4 pennies per team

Setup

Divide students into teams and give each team 4 pennies. Position the teams at opposite ends of the table. Flip a coin to see which team goes first.

How to Play

This game is like boccie ball but uses pennies instead of balls. The game begins with any player sliding the nickel toward the other end of the table. Player 1 from Team A then slides a penny, face down, trying to get close to the nickel. Player 1 from Team B slides a penny, face up, trying to get close to the nickel. Alternating between teams, each player continues until all pennies have been used. If a penny bumps the nickel into a new location, that's fine. Players may also slide their pennies to bump the other team's pennies away from the nickel.

At the end of the round, the team with the closest penny gets 1 point and gets to start the next round by sliding the nickel. If 2 or more pennies are equally close, each penny gets 1 point. The first team to score 10 points wins.

Safety Considerations

Do not allow players to run around the table.

Teaching Tips

Make this game more challenging by playing on the floor—a long hallway would be best. The larger the playing area, the more challenging the game.

BANK DEPOSIT

Number of Participants	Grade Level	Activity Level	Playing Area
2 players per game	4 and above	Low	Long table or smooth floor

Recommended Equipment

- 1 nickel per player
- 1 dime per player
- 1 water-soluble marker

Setup

Draw a 2-inch (5-centimeter) square in the middle of the table; this is the "bank." Position 2 students at opposite ends of a table. In front of each player, place a nickel 2 inches (5 centimeters) away from the edge of the table. Place a dime between the table edge and the nickel.

How to Play

Players take turns flicking their dimes to bump their nickels toward the bank. On each subsequent turn, coins are played wherever they land. (If a coin falls off the table, return it to the spot where it fell). The first player to bump the nickel all the way into the bank—it must land inside the square without touching any lines—is the winner.

Safety Considerations

To prevent sore fingers, warn students not to flick their fingers against the table edge.

Teaching Tips

Make the game more challenging by adding a robber.

Bank Robber

In this game, players get to divert their opponent's coins. After two flicks each, players become "robbers" and get to flick their opponent's dime once. Robbers can try to bump their opponent's nickel away from the bank or flick their opponent's dime further away from the nickel.

HEADS UP

Number of Participants	Grade Level	Activity Level	Playing Area
2 to 10 players per group	4 and above	Low	Large table or flat surface

Recommended Equipment

- ⊙ 1 penny per player

Setup

Have students stand around a table (or sit on the floor in a circle) facing each other. Give each student 1 penny.

How to Play

Players place a penny in their palms and, in unison, turn their hands over and smack them onto the table (the penny should land between the table and their palms). Players lift up their hands simultaneously, leaving their pennies on the table. If the number of heads showing equals the number of tails showing, everyone picks up their coins and plays again. If there are fewer heads than tails, the heads get 1 point. If there are fewer tails, the tails get 1 point. After 10 rounds, the player with the most points wins.

Safety Considerations

To prevent sore hands, warn students not to smack their hands on the table too hard.

Teaching Tips

In the case of a tie, have the tying students play another round, and another, until the tie is broken.

TIC-TAC-TOE

Number of Participants	Grade Level	Activity Level	Playing Area
2 players per game	4 and above	Low	Large table or smooth floor

Recommended Equipment

- ◎ 4 quarters per player
- ◎ Water-soluble marker

Setup

Draw a tic-tac-toe grid at the end of a long table (preferably 2 yards [meters] long). Each square should be approximately 4 inches (10 centimeters). Give each player 4 quarters. Flip a coin to determine who starts.

How to Play

The object of the game is to get 3 quarters in a row (horizontally, vertically, or diagonally) in the tic-tac-toe grid. (To keep track of which quarter belongs to whom, 1 player should slide his quarters heads up, and the other player should slide her quarters tails up.)

Player 1 slides his quarter into the grid. To count, quarters must land clearly in the grid without touching any lines. Otherwise, he picks up his quarter and the next player goes. Player 2 then slides her quarter, and so on. Once a quarter has successfully landed in a square, it cannot be removed. If it is knocked out of its square by another quarter, it is returned to the square it occupied.

The player who gets 3 coins in a row wins the game. In the case of a "cats" game, when no one can win, the quarters are retrieved and a new game begins. The first player to win 3 games wins the match.

Safety Considerations

Do not allow students to run around the table.

Teaching Tips

Make the game easier by drawing a larger grid, using smaller coins, and having players stand closer to the grid (or moving the grid closer to the edge of the table). Make the game more challenging by making the grid smaller and increasing the distance players must slide their quarters.

HIDDEN TREASURE

Number of Participants	Grade Level	Activity Level	Playing Area
5 to 10 students per group	4 and above	Low	Anywhere

Recommended Equipment

⊙ 2 coins per group

Setup

Ask 1 student from each group to volunteer to be in the middle. Have the rest of the group sit in a circle, facing the student in the middle, with their hands making a fist on their knees. Give a coin to 2 students in each group.

How to Play

The player in the middle closes his eyes and counts to 5 while the other players pass the 2 coins around the circle. After the count of 5, the player in the middle opens his eyes and tries to guess who has one of the coins. If he guesses correctly, he switches places with the player holding the coin and a new game begins. If he guesses incorrectly, he closes his eyes, counts to 5, and guesses again. If he guesses incorrectly five times in a row, a different student volunteers to be in the middle and the game begins again.

Safety Considerations

Do not allow students to touch or play tricks on the players in the middle when their eyes are closed.

Teaching Tips

Make the game more challenging by using only 1 coin, or by requiring players in the middle to guess which player has the coin and in which hand she is holding it.

NICKEL BASEBALL

Number of Participants	Grade Level	Activity Level	Playing Area
2 players per game	8 and above	Low	Large, flat table

Recommended Equipment

- 4 nickels per game
- 1 score pad per game

Setup

Use nickels to represent first, second, and third bases (approximately 20 inches [50 centimeters] apart), in the shape of a baseball diamond. Designate the table corner home plate—no coin needed. Divide students into teams and flip a coin to see who in each group goes first. Decide ahead of time whether you will play 5, 7, or 9 innings.

How to Play

The player who wins the coin toss is first at bat. The batter flicks a nickel from home plate, trying to hit one of the bases. If she hits first or third base, she gets a single hit. If she hits second, she gets a double. If she bumps first or third base off the table, she gets a triple. If she hits second base off the table, she scores a home run. The defensive player (the one not at bat) retrieves the nickel, keeps the bases in proper alignment, tallies each hit, and keeps score.

Players advance by being forced to the next base. If Runner 1 is on second base and the player hits a single, for example, Runner 1 stays on second and Runner 2 (the single just hit) goes to first. If the player hits another single, there will be runners at first, second, and third. If a batter does not hit a base in three consecutive tries, it is 1 out. When a batter gets 3 outs, the other player goes to bat. After 5, 7, or 9 innings, the player with the most runs wins.

Safety Considerations

To prevent sore fingers, warn students not to flick their fingers against the table edge. Do not allow students to throw the coins or flick them at one another.

Teaching Tips

If students are getting hits too easily, move the bases farther away from home plate. If it is too difficult to get a hit, move the bases closer to home.

This is a great game in the fall around World Series time.

PENNY FOOTBALL

Number of Participants	Grade Level	Activity Level	Playing Area
2 players per game	8 and above	Low	Table*

*approximately 1 yard (meter) wide (lunchroom tables work well)

Recommended Equipment

○ 1 penny per game

Setup

Pair off students. Seat players on opposite sides of the table, facing their opponents. Toss a coin to determine who starts. Give the starting players 1 penny.

How to Play

The starter (offense) places the penny on his side of the table, on the edge, to start the game. He gets to hit the penny four times (or three using Canadian rules)—these are the downs—in an effort to move the penny into his opponent's (defense) "end zone." To count as a touchdown, worth 6 points, the penny must be hanging over the table edge. The defense then places her hands on the table edge, thumbs up, to simulate the uprights. The offense takes the penny back to his own table edge and flicks it to score a 1-point conversion. To try for a 2-point conversion, he places the penny in the middle of the table and tries, in 1 hit, to get it to hang over his opponent's table edge.

If, after the second down, he does not think he can make a touchdown, he may attempt a field goal, worth 3 points. The defense sets up the uprights, with her thumbs up at the table edge. The offense flips the penny at the place it landed on the second down and then, by putting his hands in a praying position and pinching the penny between his thumbs, attempts to flip it through the uprights.

The defense then becomes the offense and play continues. At the end of the game, the player with the most points wins.

Rules

- If a penny goes off the table edge during a touchdown attempt, it's the defense's turn.
- If the offense fails to score after the fourth down, the defense takes over where the coin landed (unless it went off the table, in which case the defense gets the ball and starts from her own end zone).

Safety Considerations

Warn students to protect their eyes by moving their head to the side during conversion and field goal attempts.

Teaching Tips

This can be a fun game at the end of the regular football season or during the Superbowl.

DIME SOCCER

Number of Participants	Grade Level	Activity Level	Playing Area
2 players per game	4 and above	Low	Large table

Recommended Equipment

- 7 dimes per game

Setup

Pair off students and seat them opposite each other along the sides of the table. Have each student use 2 dimes to mark a 4-inch (10-centimeter) goal. Flip a coin to see who starts in each group.

How to Play

Using the other 3 dimes, the starter makes a triangle on her own side, with 1 dime hanging over the table edge in her goal. She then shoots this dime (kicks the ball) between the other 2 to advance downfield. (The dime being shot is the ball.) To score a goal, she kicks the ball through her opponent's goalposts.

Players can continue to advance the ball as long as they can kick it between the other 2 dimes. If at any time the ball does not go between the 2 dimes, or if any of the dimes go off the table, opponents get to start by placing their 3 dimes in a triangle, with 1 dime hanging over the table edge, and so on. At the end of the game, the player who scores the most goals wins.

Safety Considerations

To prevent sore fingers, warn students not to hit the edge of the table on their first kick.

Teaching Tips

Make the game easier or more challenging by adjusting the size of the goal.

QUARTER HOCKEY

Number of Participants	Grade Level	Activity Level	Playing Area
2 students per game	4 and above	Low	Large table

Recommended Equipment

- 2 quarters per game
- 1 nickel per game

Setup

Mark 4-inch (10-centimeter) goals at opposite sides of the table. Pair off students and seat them opposite each other. Place 1 nickel between each pair of students (along the middle of the table) and 1 quarter on each table edge (in front of every student). Flip a coin to determine who will start the game.

How to Play

One at a time, players try to score using their quarters (their sticks) to move the nickel (the puck) into their opponent's goal. Players may use their sticks to hit the puck or their opponent's stick. If the puck or a stick goes off the table, it is placed on the table edge where it fell off.

When a player makes a goal, the puck is placed in the middle of the table and play resumes. At the end of the game, usually 5 minutes, the player who scored the most goals wins.

Safety Considerations

To reduce the risk of eye injuries, students should slide their coins across the table, not flip them.

Teaching Tips

Make the game easier or more difficult by adjusting the goal size.

COIN GOLF

Number of Participants	Grade Level	Activity Level	Playing Area
2 to 4 players per game	4 and above	Low	Large table or smooth floor

Recommended Equipment

- 1 quarter per game
- 1 penny per player
- Objects to be used as obstacles (books, rulers, pens, and so on)

Setup

Set a quarter (the hole) at the far end of the table and place obstacles (sand traps, hills, and so on) between the quarter and the opposite side (tee-off area). Divide students into groups and flip a coin to see who will start. Distribute pennies to starters.

How to Play

The starter places a penny (the ball) in the tee-off area and then proceeds down the course by flicking it to advance toward the hole, avoiding all obstacles along the way. Once on the green, the player putts by flicking the penny to hit the quarter. Then the next player proceeds down the course, starting at the tee-off area and so on.

Each flick counts as 1 stroke. If the ball goes off the course, it is positioned where it went off and the player takes a 2-stroke penalty. If the ball hits an obstacle, the player takes a 1-stroke penalty. The player with the fewest strokes wins that hole and gets to design the next hole by rearranging the obstacles. After 9 holes, the player with the lowest overall score wins the game.

Safety Considerations

Do not allow students to run around the table.

Teaching Tips

For large classes, you'll need several tables. (Groups should each have their own course.) If you had 9 tables, or a large enough floor, you could design a different layout for each hole and players could advance through the entire course one hole at a time.

PENNY BASKETBALL

Number of Participants	Grade Level	Activity Level	Playing Area
2 players per game	4 and above	Low	Large table

Recommended Equipment

- 3 pennies per game

Setup

Pair off students and position them opposite each other at the table. Flip a coin to see who starts in each group and give the starters 3 pennies.

How to Play

The starter (offense) places 3 pennies in the shape of a triangle, with 1 of the pennies hanging over the edge of the table at her end. She then shoots this penny between the other 2 to advance down the court. (The penny being shot is the ball.) As long as she can shoot the ball between the other 2 pennies, she may continue. If the ball does not go between the 2 pennies, or if any of the pennies goes off the table, it's the opponent's (defense) turn.

To score a basket, the offense shoots the ball into the defense's basket. Defensive players form baskets with their thumbs and index fingers together (see illustration). Offensive players shoot the ball by pinching the ball between their thumbs (see illustration).

At the end of the game, the player who made the most baskets wins.

Safety Considerations

Warn defensive players to protect their eyes by moving their head to the side when the offense is shooting a basket.

Teaching Tips

If students get too rambunctious when shooting their baskets, or if you want to avoid all temptation in the first place, use quarters as the baskets. Position two quarters on opposite sides of the table and then players must shoot the ball between the other 2 pennies and hit the quarter to score.

A QUARTER AMONG FRIENDS

Number of Participants	Grade Level	Activity Level	Playing Area
3 or more teams of 15 to 60 players	4 and above	Low	Anywhere

Recommended Equipment

- ⊙ 1 quarter
- ⊙ 1 blindfold per team

Setup

Divide students into teams and blindfold 1 player from each team. Arrange all players in a large circle facing the center. Place the quarter in the middle of the circle.

How to Play

At the command to start, players gently spin their blindfolded teammate around three times and point them toward the middle of the circle. They then direct their blindfolded teammate toward the quarter. No one is allowed to touch the blindfolded players, and only blindfolded players are allowed to move within the circle. The team whose blindfolded player picks up the quarter wins the game.

Safety Considerations

To prevent falls, do not allow students to spin blindfolded teammates too quickly. To prevent mid-circle collisions, instruct blindfolded players not to move abruptly inside the circle.

Teaching Tips

To add to the confusion and excitement of the game, alternate players from other teams when forming the circle—for example, Player 1 from Team A stands next to Player 1 from Team B, followed by Player 2 from Team A and then Player 1 from Team C, and so on.

Give students time between games to develop strategies. Although the game is more entertaining to watch when all students are shouting out directions, teammates will soon realize that it is more effective if only 1 teammate speaks.

Using a tennis ball in place of the quarter adds a fun dimension to this game, because the ball may roll or be kicked by a blindfolded student.

chapter 3

Group Games

CROTCHETY PIPE WALK

Number of Participants	Grade Level	Activity Level	Playing Area
5 to 8 players per team	8 and above	Medium	Large flat area*

*a volleyball court would be sufficient for 2 teams

Recommended Equipment

- 1 plastic pipe (3 yards [meters] long, 2 inches [5 centimeters] wide) per team
- 2 pylons per team
- 1 bench per 2 teams

Setup

Set up side-by-side obstacle courses using the pylons, bench, and other obstacles. (Place the bench so that both teams can cross it during the race.) Divide students into teams and line up each team in single file, their legs spread slightly. Have team members place the plastic pipe between their legs.

How to Play

Teams walk around an obstacle course, going completely around the pylons and over the bench along the way, without touching the pipe with their hands. If any player loses contact with the team or the pipe during the race, the whole team must start over. The first team to complete the obstacle course wins.

Safety Considerations

Instruct players not to step on the benches. Teams should cross each bench slowly so that it does not fall over.

Teaching Tips

The obstacle courses can be made more complicated for older students and simpler for younger students.

THE GREAT ESCAPE

Number of Participants	Grade Level	Activity Level	Playing Area
Teams of 5 to 15 players	8 and above	Medium	Beach or padded surface

Recommended Equipment

- 1 post (4 × 4 inchs and 8 feet long [10 × 10 cm and 8 meters long])
- 20 yards (meters) of rope per team
- 4 sticks, approximately 2 yards (meters) long, per team

Setup

To designate each team's area, secure 4 sticks in the sand approximately 5 yards (meters) apart. String a rope around them just below shoulder height of the shortest player in the class. (The area between the rope and the surface is the electric fence.) Divide students into teams, giving a 4 × 4 to each, and have each team stand inside its own fenced area.

How to Play

The object of the game is to transport each team member over the electric fence without touching or going under the rope. If a team member or the 4 × 4 touches the electric fence, the whole team must go back inside the fenced area and start again. The first team to successfully escape wins.

Safety Considerations

To prevent neck or other bodily injury, do not allow students to dive over the fence. Before each game, inspect the 4 × 4s for slivers.

Teaching Tips

Teams will typically form a pyramid to get the first few players over the fence and have the lightest players be the last to escape by walking up the 4 × 4 (held by team members on the other side of the fence) and jumping over the fence. If you have an extremely overweight student in class, however, you might want to allow each team to start with 1 player outside the fence.

LIMITED CONTACTS

Number of Participants	Grade Level	Activity Level	Playing Area
5 to 25 players per team	4 and above	Medium	Anywhere

Recommended Equipment

⊙ None

Setup

Draw 2 parallel lines, approximately 4 yards (meters) apart, on the floor. Divide students into teams and line them up behind one of the lines.

How to Play

The object of the game is to get from one line to the other in a certain number of moves and using a certain number of body contacts on the ground. Team members must stay in touch with each other, moving as a unit, and are only allowed to be in contact with the ground at a certain number of points. The body parts that are in contact with the ground cannot be alternated for other body parts. For example, if 10 players were on each team, and you allowed 10 points of contact, they could all link arms and hop across on 1 foot (to walk across on both feet they would need 20 points of contact).

Reduce the number of contacts by 1 each round—to 9, then to 8, and so on. The first team to complete the last round (in the fewest moves and with the fewest number of body contact points) wins.

Safety Considerations

To prevent falls, do not allow students to sit on one another's shoulders.

Teaching Tips

To make the game more challenging, draw the lines further apart. You can also specify body parts. For example, tell students they must get from one line to the other without using their feet (they could slide on their rears or walk on their knees).

YING, YANG, YOU, BACK

Number of Participants	Grade Level	Activity Level	Playing Area
5 to 25 students per group	8 and above	Low	Anywhere

Recommended Equipment

⊙ None

Setup

Position students in a circle, each facing the center. Designate a player to start the game.

How to Play

The starter places her hand over her head, points to a player beside her (right hand points to the player on the left, left hand points to the player on the right) and shouts, "Ying!" The player she pointed to responds immediately by pointing across her waist at another player and shouting, "Yang!" This player immediately extends his arm, points to someone across the circle and shouts, "You!" That player then "yings" a player on the left or right, who "yangs" the next player, who "yous" the next player, and so on.

If players hesitate, do not call out the correct word (*ying*, *yang*, or *you*), or point incorrectly, they are out and sit in the middle of the circle. Another player begins and play continues until 1 player is left. That last remaining player is the winner.

Safety Considerations

Position students far enough apart so that they don't elbow each other in the face.

Teaching Tips

Start slowly. Once students get the hang of it, speed up the pace. Once students have mastered the game, add a variation. The

game proceeds as described previously, but at each "you" call in the sequence, there are two options. "You'd" players may (1) "ying" a player next to them, or (2) they may block the call by crossing their forearms in front of their faces and shouting, "Back!" at which point the player who shouted "you!" must "ying" a player beside them. These sequences would proceed as follows: (1) "Ying!" "Yang!" "You!" "Ying!" and so on; (2) "Ying!" "Yang!" "You!" "Back!" "Ying!" and so on.

TRIATHLON

Number of Participants	Grade Level	Activity Level	Playing Area
1 to 4 players per team	4 and above	High	gymnasium or hallway

Recommended Equipment

- 2 scooters per player
- 1 tricycle per team
- 2 pieces of carpet per team

  ⊙ 4 pylons

  ⊙ 1 stopwatch per team

Setup

Position 4 pylons to demarcate the course. (These pylons can designate inside or outside boundaries.) Line up students behind the starting line, or divide them into teams and line up teams behind the starting line.

How to Play

This is a timed race to see how quickly a team (or player) can complete three events:

1. Swimming. Lying on 2 scooters, players swim once around the course by propelling themselves with their hands.

2. Biking. Players ride tricycles once around the course.

3. Running. Players go once around the course by shuffling their feet on 2 small pieces of carpet.

Safety Considerations

Provide sufficient space between walls and pylons so that students do not crash into the wall as they turn the corner to complete the lap. Likewise, make the courses wide enough that students do not crash into one another during the biking and swimming events.

Teaching Tips

If students are competing in teams, each player can complete all three events before the next player goes or team members can complete one event at a time. For example, Teammate 1 swims once around the course, then Teammate 2 swims once around the course, and so on, followed by Teammate 1 biking once around the course, then Teammate 2 biking once around the course, and so on. If you divide students into teams of 3 players, each teammate can race a different event within the triathlon.

GOING NUTS

Number of Participants	Grade Level	Activity Level	Playing Area
5 to 8 players per team	4 and above	Low	Anywhere

Recommended Equipment

- 1 threaded bar (a big bolt with no head), approximately 1 yard (meter) long, per team
- 1 nut per player

Setup

Divide students into teams. Screw 1 nut per team member into the middle of each threaded bar and give 1 bar to each team.

How to Play

At the signal to start, teams try to remove the nuts from the bar. The first team that successfully removes all of the nuts from the bar wins.

Safety Considerations

Warn students to be careful not to drop the bar on anyone's toes.

Teaching Tips

Let students figure out the quickest way to remove the nuts from the bar (1 or 2 team members should hold the bar while the others unscrew the nuts).

If the nuts get too close to each other, they'll jam. Students will need to screw them in opposite directions to get them apart.

To keep track of the nuts, have students race to screw the nuts back to the middle of the bar as the next game.

BALLOONS AWAY

Number of Participants	Grade Level	Activity Level	Playing Area
5 or more students per game	1 and above	Medium	Any defined area

Recommended Equipment

- 2 balloons per player

Setup

Have students blow up 2 balloons and spread out in the playing area.

How to Play

At the signal to start, players toss all the balloons up in the air. From that point, players hit the balloons to keep them afloat. Balloons may only be hit—not caught or held. If a balloon touches the ground, the nearest player tosses it back into the air and gets 1 point. If players catch or hold a balloon, they also get 1 point. At the end of the game (usually 2 to 3 minutes), the player with the fewest points wins.

Safety Considerations

Use nonallergenic balloons.

Teaching Tips

Make the game more challenging by adding balloons (students get 3 or 4 balloons each). To simplify the game for younger students, you may want to start with 1 balloon per student.

BALLOON STOMP

Number of Participants	Grade Level	Activity Level	Playing Area
2 teams of 5 to 10 players	4 and above	Medium	Anywhere*

*a basketball court works well

Recommended Equipment

⊙ 20 balloons

Setup

Divide the playing area with a centerline and demarcate the safety zones—the area between the wall and the end line of each court half. Divide students into 2 teams and position each team on opposite halves of the court. Have students blow up the balloons and place 3 balloons in each team's safety zone. (The other 14 balloons are replacements.)

How to Play

At the signal to start, players run across the court and try to pop the other team's balloons by stomping on them. At the same time, players try to prevent opponents from entering their safety zone and popping their balloons. Players are safe in their own half of the court and once they are in the other team's safety zone. If tagged on the other team's court outside the safety zone, however, players must return to their own half.

Each popped balloon is worth 1 point. When a balloon is popped, a replacement balloon is placed in the safety zone and the player who popped the balloon returns to her half of the court before resuming play again. At the end of the game, when all replacement balloons have been used and one team's balloons have all been popped, the team with the most points wins.

Safety Considerations

Make sure that balloon fragments are cleaned up so that students do not slip on them. Also, be sure to use nonallergenic balloons.

Students frightened by loud noises may need to be excused during this activity.

Teaching Tips

Make the game more challenging by having students who are tagged on the other team's side sit down and remain seated until they are tagged by a teammate, at which point they can resume play without walking back to their own half.

WHEELING AROUND

Number of Participants	Grade Level	Activity Level	Playing Area
5 or more players per game	8 and above	Medium	Gymnasium or other walled area

Recommended Equipment

○ None

Setup

Have students stand in a large circle, each facing the middle and holding hands with the players beside them, to form a wheel. One player's back should be against a wall.

How to Play

Starting against the wall, students rotate to the left or right, making the wheel roll around the gym walls. The challenge is to maintain the shape of a circle and always have 1 point of contact with the wall. The object of the game is to successfully roll around the entire gym once.

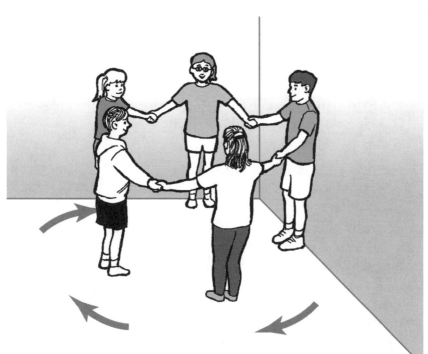

Safety Considerations

Remind students that this is not a race. Roll the wheel slowly to prevent the risk of students tripping and falling.

Teaching Tips

To make things more interesting, divide students into smaller groups and have several wheels rolling around the walls in different directions. This will mean rolling around other wheels as well as the walls. You could also have some fun with this game by moving students outside and rolling around the perimeter of the school building (watch out for flower beds).

FRISBEE GOLF

Number of Participants	Grade Level	Activity Level	Playing Area
Up to 18 groups*	8 and above	Medium	Outdoors**

*of 1 to 4 players, a maximum of 72 players on an 18-hole course
**on a large field (a treed area is best)

Recommended Equipment

- 1 Frisbee per player (if possible, as many colors as players in each group)
- 9 or 18 hula hoops
- 2 pylons per hole

Setup

Place hula hoops (these are the "holes") in strategic locations around a field to make a 9- or 18-hole course. On a piece of paper, designate the sequence of the holes as well as a throw-off area for each. Use 2 pylons to mark the throw-off area for each hole. Divide students into groups, distribute the Frisbees, and have each group go to a throw-off area. (If using groups of 2, 3, or 4 players, use different-colored Frisbees to avoid confusion.) Use a whistle or other loud signal to start the game.

How to Play

At the signal to start, players take turns tossing their Frisbees from the throw-off areas, in the direction of their first hole. After the first Frisbee toss, players walk down the fairway to the location of their Frisbee and throw it again, moving closer to the hole. Golf etiquette states that the player farthest from the hole throws first, before other players have passed. (This also makes for safer Frisbee golfing.) Each throw counts as 1 stroke.

Players continue to throw until their Frisbees land and stay inside the hula hoop. Players then tally their strokes and advance to the next hole on the course. (Players who start at the last hole advance to the first hole.) At the end of the round (9 or 18 holes), the player with lowest score (fewest strokes) wins.

Safety Considerations

Make sure students watch out for one another when tossing their Frisbees. (You might want to impose penalty strokes if students hit others.)

Teaching Tips

Students can tally their scores individually or as teams (total strokes of all teammates).

In addition, try some of these variations to Frisbee Golf.

Best Ball

Every student in the group throws from where the best throw landed.

Soccer Golf

Students kick soccer balls into each hula hoop.

Beanbag Golf

Students toss beanbags into the hula hoops. This is an excellent variation for younger children or for playing indoors. Because beanbags do not travel as far as soccer balls or Frisbees, the hoops should be closer together.

BOOR'S ULTIMATE MEDICAL DODGEBALL

Number of Participants	Grade Level	Activity Level	Playing Area
2 teams of 5 to 12 players	8 and above	Medium	Basketball court

Recommended Equipment

- ◉ 4 mats per team (either 3 blue and 1 red, or 3 red and 1 blue)
- ◉ 9 soft balls (4 white, 2 yellow, 1 green, and 2 blue)

Setup

Select 2 students, or ask for volunteers, to referee the game. Divide remaining students into 2 teams and position them on opposite sides of the court. Give each team 4 mats—either 3 blue and 1 red, or 3 red and 1 blue. (The 3 mats are buildings and the 1 mat is a hospital.) Have students set up their buildings and hospital.

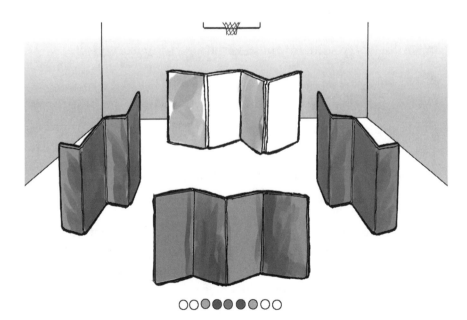

○○○●●●●○○

Place the balls (4 white, 2 yellow, 2 blue, and 1 green) on the centerline and line up students along the wall of their own half of the court.

How to Play

The object of the game is to "knock down" opponents, their buildings, and their hospital, either by hitting them with a ball or by making a basket with the green or blue balls in the opponent's half of the court. At the signal to start, players run and try to get a ball. Players throw the balls at their opponents and the opposing team's buildings, trying to knock the buildings down. Players also try to sink either the yellow, blue, or green ball into the opposing team's basket.

At the end of the game (usually 20 minutes), the team with the most players and buildings standing wins the game. Winning 2 out of 3 games wins the match.

Rules

- Players cannot cross the centerline during the game.
- Any ball (yellow, blue, green, or white) can hit players or buildings to knock them down.

Players

- All balls must be thrown at players below the waist.
- When hit by a fly ball (i.e., the ball does not bounce on the floor), players must immediately sit down, drop any balls they have in their hands, and wait for a teammate (medic) to escort them to the hospital.
- When a player catches a ball thrown by an opponent, that opponent must sit and wait for a teammate (medic) to escort them to the hospital.
- If a player tries to catch a ball thrown by an opponent but fumbles the ball, that player must sit and wait for a teammate (medic) to escort them to the hospital.
- If the ball hits a teammate before it is caught, that teammate does not have to sit down; instead, the player who threw it

must sit down and wait for a teammate (medic) to escort them to the hospital.

- Players may have only 1 ball at a time and must throw it within 5 seconds or they will have to sit.

Baskets

- If a team shoots a blue basket (a basket shot with a blue ball), all of the opponents' buildings, except the hospital, are knocked down.
- If a team shoots a yellow basket, that team's downed buildings (except hospitals) are automatically repaired and can be stood back up.
- The team that shoots a green basket automatically wins and the game is over.

Buildings

- Players cannot touch their buildings at any point during the game—unless a yellow ball has been sunk. If any player touches a building, the building goes down.
- Once a building is knocked down, it stays down until it is rebuilt (a yellow basket must be shot).
- Once the hospital is knocked down, it stays down for the remainder of the game and sitting players may not rejoin the game.

Hospital

- Hit players must be escorted to the hospital; they cannot go alone.
- Once at the hospital, players slowly count to 3 and are then free to play.

Safety Considerations

Make sure that students aim balls below the waist.

Teaching Tips

Younger students may find this game difficult because strategy is so important. For example, a team can almost assure victory by knocking down the opponent's hospital. (No players will be able to rejoin the game once they've been hit.) Thus, setting up buildings to protect the hospital is a good idea. Use discretion in revealing strategy. Some students may find the challenge of devising their own strategy more exciting.

Because there is so much action in this game, referees will need to carefully watch for players supporting their buildings, not waiting for a medic, and so on.

ABS ROLLERBALL

Number of Participants	Grade Level	Activity Level	Playing Area
3 or more teams	8 and above	Medium	Anywhere

Recommended Equipment

- 100 feet of 1/2-inch ABS plastic pipe per team
- 1 ball bearing per team

Setup

Divide students into teams. Give each team a pipe wound up in a coil and a ball bearing.

How to Play

The object of the game is to be the first to move the ball bearing from one end of the pipe to the other (if you have only 1 pipe, time the event).

At the signal to start, teams spread out around the room, holding their pipe at different heights to keep the ball bearing rolling. Once in position, a team member places the ball bearing in the pipe. When the team member at the other end of the pipe catches the ball bearing (the fastest times average around 8 seconds) the race is over. The first team to catch the ball bearing wins.

Safety Considerations

Watch that students don't get too rambunctious and knock each other down with the pipe.

Teaching Tips

To make cleanup fast and fun, see which team can wind the pipe up in a coil first.

This game has many possible variations. A simple adaptation is to challenge students to see how quickly they can move a ball bearing from one end of the pipe to the other end, and then back again. (This will require some height adjustment and repositioning of the pipe.) Another simple adaptation is to add a second and third ball bearing, 5 seconds apart. The winner is the team that gets all 5 ball bearings out first.

You might also want to try the following variations (and add your own):

Coiled Rollerball

Keep the pipe wound in a coil and see how quickly only 1 player can move the pipe to get the ball bearing around.

Straight Rollerball

Uncoil the pipe and have the team hold it in a straight line. See how quickly they can move the ball bearing through the pipe.

Uphill Rollerball

Find a small hill and challenge students to get the ball bearing, through the pipe, from the bottom to the top of the hill.

No-Hands Rollerball

Try any of these variations but with no hands.

JJ BOWLING

Number of Participants	Grade Level	Activity Level	Playing Area
6 players per lane	8 and above	Low	Bowling alley

Recommended Equipment

- 1 bowling ball and pair of shoes per player (alley will provide)
- 1 blindfold per team

How to Play

Like traditional bowling, the object of the game is to knock down as many pins as possible and score the most points. Unlike traditional bowling, bowlers must throw the ball differently each frame.

- Frame 1: Throw the ball granny style (forward through the legs).
- Frame 2: Hop to the line on the left foot and throw the ball with both hands.
- Frame 3: Lay on the floor and push the ball with both hands.
- Frame 4: Hop to the line on both feet and throw the ball with both hands.
- Frame 5: Throw the ball with the left hand.
- Frame 6: Throw the ball with the right hand.
- Frame 7: Throw the ball blindfolded (a partner can help on this frame).
- Frame 8: Throw the ball backward through the legs.
- Frame 9: Lay on the floor and push the ball with both feet.
- Frame 10: Hop to the line on the right foot and throw the ball with the left hand.

Safety Considerations

Warn students to watch their toes, as well as their teammates'.

Teaching Tips

Be creative and design other ways to make each frame entertaining and challenging.

HOOP ESCAPE

Number of Participants	Grade Level	Activity Level	Playing Area
10 to 20 players per team	8 and above	Medium	Large, open area

Recommended Equipment

- 1 hula hoop, approximately 2 yards (meters) in diameter, per team

Setup

Divide students into teams and distribute 1 hula hoop to each.

How to Play

One team member pushes the hula hoop, and as it is rolling, the rest of the teammates must go through the hoop, one by one, before it falls to the ground. The first team to get everyone through the hoop before it falls down wins. Team members need to decide how best to line everyone up to succeed at this event.

Safety Considerations

Be sure students don't run into each other when 2 hoops roll close together.

Teaching Tips

It will undoubtedly take several attempts to succeed at this task. Encourage students to brainstorm effective lineups and strategies between rounds. If 1 team continually wins, challenge them to find a more efficient way of getting through the hoop.

CRABS AWAY

Number of Participants	Grade Level	Activity Level	Playing Area
2 teams of 8 to 25 players	4 and above	Medium	Anywhere

Recommended Equipment

⊙ None

Setup

Delineate end lines on the playing field, approximately 9 yards (meters) apart. (The end lines on a volleyball court work well.) Divide students into teams. Then divide each team in half, creating an offensive line and a defensive line. Have each team sit on opposite sides of the playing field, behind their end line.

How to Play

At the signal to start, the offense tries to cross the other team's end line while the defense tries to prevent the other team's offense from crossing their line. Players move by walking like a crab—their backs toward the ground, moving on hands and feet, in the direction of their feet. Each player who makes it across the other team's end line scores 1 point.

Rules

⊙ Players may move forward only. Moving backward (head first) is not allowed.

⊙ Defensive players can block approaching crabs but may not hold them.

⊙ No kicking is allowed.

After 30 seconds, points are tallied and players switch roles—the offense becomes the defense and the defense becomes the offense. After 30 seconds, points are tallied, players switch roles, and so on. After 5 rounds (1 minute per round), the team with the highest score wins.

Safety Considerations

To prevent students from banging heads, be sure to enforce the "no moving backward (head first)" rule.

Teaching Tips

This is a great game for students learning about marine life in science class.

SOCK IT TO 'EM

Number of Participants	Grade Level	Activity Level	Playing Area
4 or more players per game	4 and above	High	Padded surface*

*(such as a wrestling mat)

Recommended Equipment

⊙ None

Setup

Position students on the padded surface (if using wrestling mats, you may have to divide students into groups). Instruct students to remove their shoes and keep their socks on. (If necessary, you may have to distribute extra socks.)

How to Play

At the start signal, players try to steal other players' socks by pulling them off. Stolen socks are returned, but players may not put them back on until the start of a new game. Players crawl around the playing area on all fours. When both socks have been stolen, players are out and sit on the sidelines until the end of the game. The last player with a sock wins.

Safety Considerations

Prevent injuries by imposing a 1-sock penalty on students caught kicking or playing rough.

Teaching Tips

To speed up the game, have players start with only 1 sock. To lessen the elimination factor, allow students to play throughout the game. Have players go to the side when they lose their sock, do 10 push-ups, put their sock back on, and get back into the game.

chapter 4

Races and Relays

The real fun of relays and races is in the participation. If students have to wait too long for their turns, they will lose focus. Try to keep team sizes to a minimum: 4 to 5 participants if possible. If class size does not permit teams of equal size, some students may have to go twice (team members should decide).

When setting up these races and relays, demarcate start/finish lines far enough away from walls or other obstacles to avoid crashes, should students lose their balance or not be able to slow down quickly enough.

SWIMMING RELAY

Number of Participants	Grade Level	Activity Level	Playing Area
4 to 5 players per team	4 and above	High	Gym*

*or other area with hard, smooth floor

Recommended Equipment

- 2 scooters per team
- 1 gymnastics mat per team

Setup

Designate the "pool." This could be a volleyball court, basketball court, or any area already marked in the gym. The area immediately outside the pool is the deck. Place a gymnastics mat on top of 2 scooters—1 scooter under the front of the mat, the other under the back. Position the mats/scooters at the edge of the pool.

Divide students into teams and line up teams behind their mats/scooters.

How to Play

This is a relay race. At the signal to start, the first student in each team "swims" to the end of the pool and back. When swimming freestyle, for example, students lie face down on the mat and propel themselves forward by pushing on the floor one hand at a time. They may not use their feet for propulsion.

When swimmers get back to the starting edge of the pool, they get off their mats and sit on the deck near their team, and the next team member goes. The first team to have all swimmers complete their laps and be seated on the deck wins.

Safety Considerations

Warn students to keep their hands (and their hair) out from under scooter wheels. Also, have students remove necklaces or other dangling objects.

Teaching Tips

For more variety, try using different strokes like the butterfly or backstroke. In the butterfly, swimmers lie face down and use both hands at the same time. The backstroke is trickier. It is like the freestyle, except swimmers lie on their backs.

For even more variety, try a combination of strokes in each race. For example, have students use the butterfly on the first lap and the backstroke on the second lap.

Finally, you can divide teams in half and position half of each team on opposite ends of the pool. In this type of relay, each student swims only 1 lap and then the next team member goes. The first team to have all swimmers complete their laps and be seated on the deck (in this case, 2 decks per team, each on opposite sides of the pool) wins.

INDIANAPOLIS 500

Number of Participants	Grade Level	Activity Level	Playing Area
4 to 6 teams of 5 to 8 players	4 and above	High	Large area with a flat, hard floor

Recommended Equipment

- 2 scooters per team
- 4 pylons

Setup

In the middle of a gym, set up the track: place the pylons 4 to 6 yards (meters) from the center of the gym, forming a square. Inside the square is the pit area. Outside the square is the track. Designate a line, perhaps a centerline in the gym, to be the start/ finish line. Have 1 player (the driver) from each team sit on 2 scooters (their rears on one and their feet on the other) at the start line; this is the car. A teammate (the engine) stands behind each driver. The rest of the players stand in their assigned team location in the pit area.

How to Play

At the signal to start, the engine pushes the team car once around the track, just past the team's assigned pit area where a new engine takes over. The new engine pushes the car around the track once and the next engine takes over. The race continues until everyone has had a turn at being the engine. The last player pushes the car once around the track and over the finish line. Everyone else must be seated in the team pit area. The first car over the finish line, with all other team members seated in the pit, wins.

Safety Considerations

Participants should wear helmets, both for safety and a little realism. Make sure the corners are far enough away from the walls to prevent crashes into the walls.

Teaching Tips

If once around the track is not strenuous enough, have each engine push the car twice around the track. Another option: determine the length of the race (20 or 30 laps) beforehand. Every engine must push the car at least once around, but team members may choose their own multilap engines. For a lengthy race, it might be helpful to designate a lap counter on each team.

CHARIOT RACES

Number of Participants	Grade Level	Activity Level	Playing Area
4 to 6 teams of 5 to 8 participants	4 and above	High	Gymnasium*

*or any large area with a hard, flat floor

Recommended Equipment

- 1 rope, approximately 1 yard (meter) long, per team
- 2 scooters per team
- 4 pylons

Setup

In the middle of a gym, set up the track: place pylons 4 to 6 yards (meters) from the center of the gym, forming a square.

Inside the square is the corral. Outside the square is the track. Designate a line, perhaps a centerline in the gym, to be the start/finish line. Have 1 player (the driver) from each team sit on 2 scooters (their rears on one and their feet on the other) at the start line, holding one end of the rope; this is the chariot. A teammate (the horse) stands in front of the chariot and holds the other end of the rope. The rest of the players stand in their assigned team location in the corral.

How to Play

At the signal to start, the horses pull their chariots once around the track and just past their corral, where a new horse takes over. The new horse pulls the chariot around the track once and then the next horse takes over. The race continues until everyone has had a turn at being the horse. The last player pulls the chariot once around the track and over the finish line. Everyone else must be seated in their corral area. The first chariot to cross the finish line, with all other team members seated in the corral, wins.

Safety Considerations

To reduce the risk of injury, provide helmets for chariot riders to wear.

Teaching Tips

If scooters are too fast, particularly for younger students, you might want to try carpet riding—riders sit on 2 pieces of carpet rather than scooters. This will slow the race somewhat and will make the horses work a little harder.

CAR TROUBLE

Number of Participants	Grade Level	Activity Level	Playing Area
4 to 5 players per team	4 to 8	High	Anywhere

Recommended Equipment

- None

Setup

Delineate 2 parallel lines approximately 10 to 15 yards (meters) apart. One line is the start/finish line; the other is where players turn and go to the finish. Divide students into teams and line them up at the start line.

How to Play

One by one, players race as quickly as they can to the far line, turn around, and come back to the finish. After crossing the finish line, players sit down at the back of the line and remain seated while other players race. The first team to complete the race and be seated in line is the winner.

In this game, players are the cars and each car has some sort of car trouble.

- Car 1 has a flat tire and must hop around the course on one foot.
- Car 2 has carburetor trouble and hops on both feet: 2 hops forward and 1 hop backward, 2 hops forward and 1 hop backward, and so on.
- Car 3 loses a wheel and must race using both hands but only one foot.
- Car 4 car has trouble starting and must count backward from 20 as quickly as possible before running the course.
- Car 5 (if applicable) has trouble going up hills and must walk the course by putting one foot immediately in front of the other (toe touching heel).

Safety Considerations

To prevent trips, falls, and slips, make sure the floor is dry and clear of debris.

Teaching Tips

Be creative in coming up with other imitations of car trouble—
or see if students can come up with ideas.

REAR RACE

Number of Participants	Grade Level	Activity Level	Playing Area
5 to 25 per team*	4 and above	Medium	Anywhere**

*(smaller teams are easier)
**(preferably a clean surface)

Recommended Equipment

○ None

Setup

Delineate 2 parallel lines 5 to 10 yards (meters) apart. One line
is the start and the other is the finish. Divide students into teams
and, behind the start line, seat them in single file by team, with
legs on either side of the player in front and feet over the other
player's thighs, and hands and arms outside the legs of the player
behind.

How to Play

At the signal to start, each team scoots across the track, staying
together as a unit. The first team to the finish wins.

Safety Considerations

You may want to have players take their shoes off.

Teaching Tips

To make the race more challenging, place a pylon on the finish
line. Teams must successfully navigate around the pylon, staying together on the turn, and finish at the start line.

SORE TOE RELAY

Number of Participants	Grade Level	Activity Level	Playing Area
4 to 6 per team	4 to 8	High	Anywhere

Recommended Equipment

⊙ None

Setup

Delineate 2 parallel lines, approximately 10 yards (meters) apart. One line is the start/finish; the other is a turn-around line. Divide students into teams and line up teams, single file, behind the start line.

How to Play

At the start signal, the first player from each team hops to the turn-around line on one foot, turns around, and hops on the other foot back to the starting line. (The player has a sore right toe on the way there and a sore left toe on the way back.) When the first player crosses the finish line, the next player goes. Players must hold the "injured" foot with both hands when hopping. The first team to complete the race and be seated behind the finish line wins.

Safety Considerations

Make sure the floor is not slippery.

Teaching Tips

For more variation, add other injuries to the race or create a relay using multiple injuries. For example, with sore feet, students would have to crawl or walk on their knees without letting their feet touch the ground. With sore legs, students could roll to the other line and back.

BLOCK-HEAD RELAY

Number of Participants	Grade Level	Activity Level	Playing Area
4 to 8 per team*	4 and above	Medium	Anywhere

*even-numbered teams work best

Recommended Equipment

- 1 building block per team
- 2 pylons per team

Setup

Divide students into teams and delineate a start line. Line up teams in pairs behind the start line and, in front of each team, make a short obstacle course by placing a pylon 5 yards (meters) away and another pylon 5 yards (meters) further (10 yards [meters] from the start). Distribute 1 building block to each team. Have the first pair of players hold it between their foreheads.

How to Play

At the signal to start, each team pair moves around the pylons and returns to the start line as quickly as possible. If the block drops, the players must start over. When they successfully complete the obstacle course and return to the start, they pass the block to the next players, who race through the course with the block between their heads. The first team to complete the course and be seated behind the start line wins.

Safety Considerations

Warn students to apply gentle pressure to the block, not so much pressure that they will bang heads if the block drops.

Teaching Tips

Using a round object like a tennis ball or volleyball can make this relay more challenging. A balloon, because it gives a little, is easier to hold and thus makes the relay faster. You may also want to have players pass the block (or ball or balloon) without using their hands.

HUMAN HURDLE RACE

Number of Participants	Grade Level	Activity Level	Playing Area
4 to 15 players per team	4 and above	High	Anywhere

Recommended Equipment

⊙ None

Setup

Divide students into teams. Have each team sit in a circle, facing out with their legs together and flat on the floor (like the hub of a spoked wheel).

How to Play

At the start signal, 1 player stands up and hops over his teammates' legs (clearing one player at a time). When he is back at his original spot, he sits back down and extends his legs. As soon as the first player has jumped over the second player's legs, the second player gets up and follows the first player. When the last player has jumped over everyone's legs, and everyone is seated in her original position, the team is done. The first team seated wins.

Safety Considerations

Warn students to jump *over*—not *on*—teammates' legs. It's best if students jump over their teammates' shins because there is more space to land.

Teaching Tips

To add some challenge to the race, have students hop on one foot.

CRAZY CARPET RELAY

Number of Participants	Grade Level	Activity Level	Playing Area
4 to 5 students per team	4 and above	High	Gymnasium*

*or other area with a smooth, hard surface

Recommended Equipment

- 1 carpet square per team
- 2 pylons per team

Setup

Divide students into teams and delineate a start line. Line up teams in single file behind the start line and, in front of each team, make a short obstacle course by placing a pylon 5 yards (meters) away and another pylon 5 yards (meters) further (10 yards [meters] from the start). Distribute carpet squares and have the first player on each team kneel on the carpet behind the start line.

How to Play

At the signal to start, players pull themselves around the obstacle course using only their hands and arms. They may not push with their feet. When the first player returns to the start line, the next teammate goes. If players slide off their carpet squares, they must go back and start over. The first team to successfully navigate the course and be seated behind the start line wins.

Safety Considerations

This relay is tough on the arms, so have students warm up beforehand.

Teaching Tips

If carpet squares are not readily available, towels will work well. To make this relay easier on the arms, have students kneel on scooters and pull/push themselves around the course.

CATERPILLAR RACE

Number of Participants	Grade Level	Activity Level	Playing Area
5 to 12 players per team	4 and above	Medium	Gymnasium*

*or other long area, 15 to 25 yards (meters), with a hard floor

Recommended Equipment

- ⊙ 1 scooter per player
- ⊙ 1 pylon per team

Setup

Designate a finish line at one end of the gym and a start line halfway down the gym (a centerline would work well). Place a pylon for each team close to the other end of the gym. Divide students into teams and line up teams in single file behind the start line. Have students lie on their scooters, holding the ankles of the student in front of them to form a long caterpillar.

How to Play

At the start signal, the caterpillar moves toward the pylon, then around it, and then back to the finish line. The player at the front of the caterpillar uses her hands. The player at the end of the caterpillar uses his feet. Players in the middle help their team advance by pulling themselves forward while holding onto the ankles of the player in front of them. The first caterpillar to cross the finish line wins.

Safety Considerations

You may want to have students in the front and middle of the caterpillar—not the end—remove their shoes. Be sure students keep their hands, clothing, and hair out from underneath scooter wheels.

Teaching Tips

To slow the race and make it more strenuous, try a variation: Inchworm Race.

Inchworm Race

This race does not involve scooters. Students lie on the floor, on their bellies, clasping the ankles of their teammates to form an inchworm, and advance by inching their way across the floor. Students' clothes may get dirty in this activity; that will only add a bit of realism.

SWAMP SHOES RELAY

Number of Participants	Grade Level	Activity Level	Playing Area
5 to 8 players per team	4 and above	High	A smooth, hard surface

Recommended Equipment

◉ 2 carpet squares (the size of students' feet) per team

Setup

Delineate the "swamp" by marking 2 parallel lines, approximately 5 to 10 yards (meters) apart. Divide students into teams and line them up behind the start line. Give each team a pair of "swamp shoes" (2 carpet squares).

How to Play

The object of this relay is to transport all team members over the swamp (from one line to the other) touching the swamp with only their swamp shoes. Only players' feet can move the shoes and only 1 player at a time can "wear" them. In other words, the shoes cannot be thrown across the swamp for the next player to use.

If players touch the swampy area with anything other than their swamp shoes, they must go back and start over. The first team to make it across the swamp wins.

Safety Considerations

Students should dismount at the finish line, not be dropped off.

Teaching Tips

Allow time at the beginning of the relay for players to brainstorm how to get their teammates across the swamp. The usual pattern is for 1 student to piggyback a teammate across, then that teammate goes back to get the next teammate. Some teams elect 1 student to go back and forth, picking up a new player each time. Other teams elect their strongest teammate to carry 2 or 3 players each crossing. They move slowly, but they have to go back and forth fewer times.

Encourage students to find creative and more efficient ways of getting their teammates across or limit them to taking only 1 player at a time.

REFRIGERATOR RELAY

Number of Participants	Grade Level	Activity Level	Playing Area
4 to 8 players per team	4 and above	Medium	Anywhere

Recommended Equipment

- 1 refrigerator box (or large box) per team

Setup

Divide students into teams and delineate 2 start/finish lines. (If playing in a gym, put these lines in opposite corners of the playing area to make the race more difficult.) Divide teams in half and line up each half in opposite corners. Give each team a refrigerator box.

How to Play

The object is for team members to get from one corner to the other. This is trickier than it sounds. Players must be under their refrigerator box as they cross the playing area. More than 1 player may travel under the box at any given time. Players may also direct their teammates if they veer off course. The first team to complete the relay wins.

Safety Considerations

Because students will not be able to see when they're underneath the boxes, reduce the potential for injurious collisions by not allowing students to run.

Teaching Tips

Allow students to brainstorm the most effective method of transport—namely, to see how many can fit underneath the box—before the relay.

To make this relay more challenging, line up teams at one line and have students transport their teammates from start to finish. Like the Swamp Shoes Relay (page 83), 1 or more students must go back and forth to transport their teammates.

HUMAN OBSTACLE RACE

Number of Participants	Grade Level	Activity Level	Playing Area
5 to 20 players per team	4 and above	Medium	Anywhere

Recommended Equipment

⊙ None

Setup

Divide students into teams and line them up in single file, approximately 1 yard (meter) apart.

How to Play

At the signal to start, the last player in line leapfrogs over the next-to-last player in line, then crawls under the legs of the next player, then leapfrogs over the next, and so on, until she comes to the front of the line. (Players being leapfrogged over may help by bending down.) As soon as the next-to-last player is leapfrogged over, he leapfrogs over the player in front of him, then

A   B

goes under the legs of the next player, and so on, until he comes to the front of the line.

Players do this until everyone has completed their leapfrogs and crawls. The player who started in front should again be in the front of the line, and the player who started in back should be in the back of the line. The first team in their original lineup wins.

Safety Considerations

Be sure teammates stand far enough apart that those jumping don't land on or bump into the next student in line.

Teaching Tips

Make this race more challenging by having teams go around a rectangle, such as a badminton court.

SKIN THE SNAKE

Number of Participants	Grade Level	Activity Level	Playing Area
5 to 15 students per team	8 and above	Low	Anywhere

Recommended Equipment

- None

Setup

Divide students into teams and line up each team in single file. Have students practice the routine (see the following paragraph) a few times.

How to Play

Players bend down and reach between their legs with their right hands to grasp the left hand of the player behind them. (Players should extend their left hands forward.) The player in the back of the line sits down, then lies down, keeping her legs together and continuing to hold the right hand of the player in front of her. The rest of the team backs up with small steps. The next-to-last player sits down, then lies down, continuing to hold the right hand of the player in front of him and the left hand of the player behind him. The team backs up with small steps. This continues until everyone is lying down, holding hands.

Then the process is reversed. The last player to lie down stands up, walks forward with small steps, and pulls up the next player. This continues until everyone is standing up again. The team that "skins the snake" the fastest wins.

Safety Considerations

Stepping over students who are lying down can be tricky. Have students practice slowly first before going for speed.

Teaching Tips

To foster class spirit, bring all teams together and skin a giant snake.

BALLOON DRIBBLE RACE

Number of Participants	Grade Level	Activity Level	Playing Area
4 to 6 players per team	1 and above	Medium	Gymnasium

Recommended Equipment

○ 2 to 3 balloons per team

Setup

Delineate a start/finish and a turn-around line: 2 parallel lines approximately 10 yards (meters) apart. Divide students into teams and line them up behind the start line. Give each team 1 balloon.

How to Play

At the signal to start, the first player in line dribbles a balloon with his feet to the turn-around line and back to the start. If the balloon pops, he must start again, first by blowing up a new balloon. When he crosses the start/finish line, he sits down at the back of the line and the next player goes. The first team to complete the race and be seated behind the start line wins.

Safety Considerations

Be sure broken balloon fragments are cleaned up immediately to avoid slips and falls. Use nonallergenic balloons.

Teaching Tips

You can also use surgical gloves or other inflatable items in this race. To make the race more challenging, have students use a hockey stick to advance the balloon or dribble 2 balloons (or other inflatable items) at the same time.

BALLOON TRAIN RACE

Number of Participants	Grade Level	Activity Level	Playing Area
5 to 25 players per team	1 and above	Low	Anywhere

Recommended Equipment

- 1 balloon per player

Setup

Demarcate a start line (approximately one-third of the way across the gym) and a finish line (close to the end of the gym). Divide students into teams and line them up in single file behind the start line. Have players place their balloons between their abdomens and the backs of the players in front of them.

How to Play

At the signal to start, the team advances toward the finish line, keeping the balloons between them. Once the teams start moving, players may not touch the balloons with their hands. If a balloon falls, the entire team must go back and start over. The first team to cross the finish line wins.

Safety Considerations

Use nonallergenic balloons. Do not allow students to push one another during the race or get too rambunctious with the balloons (for example, deliberately popping the balloons near other students' ears).

Teaching Tips

Make the race more challenging by adding obstacles or requiring students to turn at the finish line. In this case, students would cross the start line to win. You may also want to explain to students that slow and steady will win over uncontrolled speed, although they will likely figure that out for themselves.

ARCHITECTS

Number of Participants	Grade Level	Activity Level	Playing Area
5 to 10 players per team	8 and above	Low	Anywhere

Recommended Equipment

- Drawing or model of an object
- 10 to 15 Lego pieces (or other building materials such as sticks, blocks, tape, and so on)

Setup

Draw or make a model of the object students will build. Divide students into teams and have each team designate an architect and a builder (the rest are laborers). Cluster students around the playing area by team. Builders should be seated 15 yards (meters) in front of the laborers, their backs toward each other. Architects sit midway between the builders and laborers, facing the same direction as the laborers. Show the model or drawing to each team's architect and distribute building materials.

How to Play

The object is to build a replica of the model. At the signal to start, 1 laborer from each team goes to the team architect, gets 1 Lego piece and instructions on what the builder should do with that piece, and then gives the Lego to the builder and repeats the architect's instructions. The laborer then returns to the group and another laborer goes to the architect to get the next piece and set of instructions. One laborer goes at a time, following the same sequence.

Once the object is built, each builder describes it to the team architect (the only one who has seen the original object) to make sure it is correct. The object that most closely resembles the original wins.

Safety Considerations

Do not allow students to run back and forth or throw the Lego pieces.

Teaching Tips

This an entertaining relay, but it also presents an opportunity to discuss the importance of clear communication.

SLALOM RACE

Number of Participants	Grade Level	Activity Level	Playing Area
4 to 5 players per team	8 and above	High	Gymnasium or area with hard surface

Recommended Equipment

- 2 scooters per team
- 2 toilet plungers per team
- 2 pylons per team

Setup

Delineate a start/finish line. Divide students (skiers) into teams and design a race course for each team using 2 pylons. (You can add other obstacles, if available.) Line up teams in single file at the start line and give 2 scooters (skis) and 2 toilet plungers (poles) to the first skiers. Skiers sit on 1 scooter and place their feet on the other, holding a plunger in each hand.

How to Play

At the signal, skiers take off, using their poles to push themselves through the course. From the start line, they ski around the first pylon, turn around the second, ski the other way around the first pylon, and return to the start/finish line. If players lose their skis or poles, they must go back and start over. Once past the finish line, skiers get off the scooters, hand the poles to the next teammate, and then go to the back of the line and sit down. The next skier sits on the scooters and proceeds through the course, and so on, until all players have completed the course. The first team to complete the course and be seated wins.

Safety Considerations

To avoid trips and falls, warn students not to lean too far back when pushing with the plungers. Be sure to line up teams far enough apart to avoid collisions.

Teaching Tips

The toilet plungers will sometimes stick to the floor, which makes it difficult to advance quickly. Thus, to avoid frustration, it's a good idea to make the course short (5 yards [meters] is probably plenty).

chapter 5

Tugs-of-War

TRADITIONAL TUG-OF-WAR

Number of Participants	Grade Level	Activity Level	Playing Area
4 or more players per team	8 and above	High	Anywhere

Recommended Equipment

- 1 tug-of-war rope

Setup

Mark a center point and 2 parallel centerlines, each 5 yards (meters) away from the center point. Lay the rope in a straight line with its center (marked with tape or a handkerchief) at the center point. Divide students into teams (2 teams per rope) and line up each team along one side of the rope.

How to Play

At the signal to start, team members start pulling. When the rope center crosses a team's centerline, that team wins.

Safety Considerations

Be sure to use a tug-of-war rope. Synthetic ropes may burst or cause rope burns. To prevent injuries, do not allow students to let go of the rope so that the other team falls.

Teaching Tips

Try the following variations to Traditional Tug-of-War.

Up-the-Creek

For some laughs and added incentive to win, some schools hold tug-of-war contests across sandy creek beds or in muddy fields. When a team starts to lose, the students in the front are in the creek or mud.

Beanbag Pickup

Rather than trying to move the rope center past the centerline, place a beanbag 2 yards (meters) behind the player on each end of the rope. Teams try to pull their opponents far enough to their side to pick up the beanbag.

TIMED TUG-OF-WAR

Number of Participants	Grade Level	Activity Level	Playing Area
4 or more students per team	4 and above	High	Anywhere

Recommended Equipment

- 1 tug-of-war rope
- 1 stopwatch

Setup

Mark a center point and lay the rope in a straight line with its center (marked with tape or a handkerchief) at the center point. Divide students into teams (2 teams per rope) and line up each team along one side of the rope.

How to Play

Students pick up the rope and gently pull it to get it tight. Then, at the signal to start, both teams try to pull their opponents toward their own side. After 30 seconds (or 1 minute, or 2 minutes, and so on), the team with the most rope on their side wins.

Safety Considerations

Be sure to use a tug-of-war rope. Synthetic ropes may burst or cause rope burns. To prevent injuries, do not allow students to let go of the rope so that the other team falls.

Teaching Tips

You will need to adjust the time to suit your students. For extra excitement, call out the passage of 10-second intervals and then count down the last 10 seconds.

ROPE RUSH

Number of Participants	Grade Level	Activity Level	Playing Area
4 or more students per team	8 and above	High	Anywhere

Recommended Equipment

- 1 tug-of-war rope

Setup

Mark a center point and 2 parallel centerlines, each 5 yards (meters) away from the center point. Lay the rope in a straight line with its center (marked with tape or a handkerchief) at the center point. Divide students into teams (2 teams per rope) and line them up several yards (meters) away from the rope.

How to Play

At the start signal, players run to the rope and begin to pull. The first team to pull the other team past the centerline on their side wins.

Safety Considerations

Make sure students do not push one another on their way to the rope. To prevent injuries, do not allow students to let go of the rope so that the other team falls.

Teaching Tips

This tug-of-war adds running speed to the mix of power and strength. To "level the playing field," you may want to have students crawl to the rope or hop on one foot.

PAUL REVERE'S TUG-OF-WAR

Number of Participants	Grade Level	Activity Level	Playing Area
4 or more students per team	8 and above	High	Anywhere

Recommended Equipment

⊙ 1 tug-of-war rope

Setup

Mark a center point and 2 parallel centerlines, each 5 yards (meters) away from the center point. Lay the rope in a straight line with its center (marked with tape or a handkerchief) at the center point. Divide students into teams (2 teams per rope) and have teammates pair up as horses and riders. Horses get down on all fours. Then riders mount their horses and pick up the rope.

How to Play

At the signal to start, players try to pull the other team past their centerline. Riders who fall off their horses or touch the ground with their feet must let go of the rope until they have remounted their horses. The first team to pull the other team to their own side wins.

Safety Considerations

Be sure to use a tug-of-war rope. Synthetic ropes may burst or cause rope burns. To prevent injuries, do not allow students to let go of the rope so that the other team falls.

Teaching Tips

This can easily become a Timed Tug-of-War (see page 96). After 30 seconds, or any length of time, the team with the most rope on their side wins.

PUSH-OF-WAR

Number of Participants	Grade Level	Activity Level	Playing Area
4 or more students per team	8 and above	High	Anywhere

Recommended Equipment

- 1 tug-of-war rope
- 1 stopwatch

Setup

Mark a straight line and lay the rope along the line. Divide students into teams (2 teams per rope) and line up each team along the entire length of one side of the rope, alernating with players from the opposing team. Have students grasp the rope with both hands.

How to Play

At the start signal, both teams try to push the rope over the other team's line. After 30 seconds, the team with the least amount of rope on their side wins.

Safety Considerations

Be sure to use a tug-of-war rope. Synthetic ropes may burst or cause rope burns.

Teaching Tips

Adjust the time to best suit your students. For extra excitement, call out 10-second intervals and count down the last 10 seconds.

4-WAY TUG-OF-WAR

Number of Participants	Grade Level	Activity Level	Playing Area
4 teams of 4 or more students	4 and above	High	Anywhere

Recommended Equipment

- 1 4-way tug-of-war rope
- 4 beanbags

Setup

If you do not have a 4-way tug-of-war rope, make one by looping 2 tug-of-war ropes together at the center. Mark a center point and lay the rope in an X with its center (marked with tape or a handkerchief) at the center point.

Divide students into teams (4 teams per rope) and line up each team along one side of the rope. Place a beanbag a few yards (meters) behind the last team member on each end of the rope.

How to Play

At the signal to start, each team pulls until the player on the end of the rope can pick up the beanbag. The first team to pick up the beanbag is the winner.

Safety Considerations

Be sure to use a tug-of-war rope. Synthetic ropes may burst or cause rope burns. To prevent injuries, do not allow students to let go of the rope so that the other teams fall.

Teaching Tips

If you play this game four times, the score will probably be 1-1-1-1 because teams typically gang up against the winner. You may want to play four times and leave it as a tie or go to a fifth game to determine the overall winner.

BACKSIDE TUG-OF-WAR

Number of Participants	Grade Level	Activity Level	Playing Area
2 students per contest	8 and above	High	Anywhere

Recommended Equipment

⊙ None

Setup

Delineate 2 parallel lines approximately 4 yards (meters) apart. Have students stand backside-to-backside between these lines. Have them bend forward and hold hands between their legs.

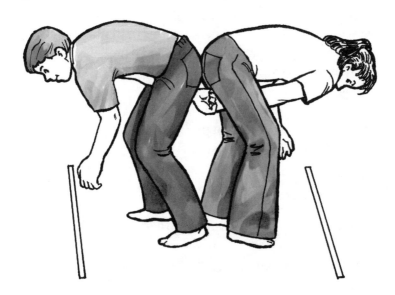

How to Play

At the signal to start, players try to pull their opponents past their line. The first one to succeed is the winner.

Safety Considerations

Do not allow students to let go of each other during the tugging.

Teaching Tips

Here is a variation you may want to try with the whole class.

Team Backside Tug-of-War

Divide the class into 2 teams and line them up between the lines. (If you have an odd number of students, try to balance teams by weight or have the "extra" student referee.) Students should stand side-by-side with their backs toward the other team. Have students bend over and, between their legs, clasp hands with the opponents behind them—right hands holding the right hands of the opposing players on their right, and left hands holding the left hands of the opposing players on their left. When executed correctly, the teams should be interlocked.

At the signal to start, students try to pull their opponents past their own team line. Either time the match (the team that pulls more of the other team to their side after 30 seconds wins), or let it run its course (the winner is the team that pulls all of the other team past their line).

CATCH-AND-PULL TUG-OF-WAR

Number of Participants	Grade Level	Activity Level	Playing Area
2 students per contest	4 and above	High	Anywhere

Recommended Equipment

○ None

Setup

Delineate a center point and 2 centerlines approximately 2 yards (meters) from the center point. Pair up players and have them face each other at the center point.

How to Play

At the signal to start, players try to grab their opponents and pull them over their centerline. The player who succeeds wins.

Safety Considerations

Warn students to grab only their opponents' arms or legs and to be careful not to bang heads.

Teaching Tips

Be sure to pair up players of similar weight.

chapter 6

Contests

Some of these contests go quickly, so it may be a good idea for students to play 2 out of 3. You can also make these contests more competitive, and add a little excitement to the class, by creating elimination tournaments. For example, if you have 32 students in class, 16 would win and 16 would lose on the first round. Have winners assemble in a separate area after each round. The winners play each other (8 matches) in the second round, leaving 8 winners and 8 losers. On the third round, 4 would win; then 2; then the overall champion. As students are eliminated, you can devise runner-up competitions for each round or have them cheer on their classmates.

SQUATTER'S RIGHTS

Number of Participants	Grade Level	Activity Level	Playing Area
2 students per contest	4 and above	Medium	Anywhere

Recommended Equipment

- 1 piece of rope, approximately 2 yards (meters) long, per contest

Setup

Pair up students. Have each student hold the opposite end of a rope and assume the squat position.

How to Play

At the signal to start, players try to pull their opponents off balance. Players lose if they let go of the rope, stand up, move one or both feet, touch the ground with either hand, or fall over.

Safety Considerations

This contest is safest when students play on a wrestling mat. Because they play in a squatting position, however, the risk of injury should be minimal.

Teaching Tips

To make this challenge more interesting, have students start by standing on one foot instead of squatting.

KANGAROO HOP

Number of Participants	Grade Level	Activity Level	Playing Area
2 students per contest	4 and above	Medium	Anywhere

Recommended Equipment

- 1 beanbag per player

Setup

Pair up students and distribute beanbags.

How to Play

Players squat and fold their arms across their chests, like kangaroos, and hold a beanbag between their knees. At the signal to start, players try to force their opponents to drop their bean-

bags, fall over, and/or unfold their arms. The kangaroo who succeeds is the winner.

Safety Considerations

This activity puts a lot of pressure on the knees, so limit the
number of rounds students play.

Teaching Tips

You can use a ball or any small object in place of the beanbag.
For added variety, try King of the Kangaroos.

King of the Kangaroos.

Unlike Kangaroo Hop, this is a group event. Students assemble,
in the starting position, in a central or defined area such as a
badminton court. At the signal, students try to get each other to
drop their beanbags, fall over, and/or unfold their arms. The
last kangaroo hopping is the winner.

STORK STAND

Number of Participants	Grade Level	Activity Level	Playing Area
2 students per contest	4 and above	Medium	Anywhere

Recommended Equipment

- None

Setup

Pair up students and have them stand on one foot, grasping each other's right hands.

How to Play

At the signal to start, players try to get their opponents to put down the other foot or move the foot they are standing on. Jiggling, bumping, pulling, pushing—any movement of the right hand and arm is allowed. The player left standing on one foot wins.

Safety Considerations

Warn students about rough play, as well as banging heads. Kicking and punching should be discouraged.

Teaching Tips

As noted at the beginning of this chapter, making this contest into a tournament could be fun for the whole class. After each round, have the winners play against each other to determine a class champion.

KNEE BOXING

Number of Participants	Grade Level	Activity Level	Playing Area
2 students per contest	4 and above	High	Anywhere

Recommended Equipment

⊙ None

Setup

Pair up students and have them stand opposite each other.

How to Play

At the start signal, players try to touch their opponent's knee with either hand. At the same time, they try to prevent their opponents from doing the same by moving their own legs and knees. The first player to touch her opponent's knee wins.

Safety Considerations

Warn students not to bang heads when they are reaching for their opponents' knees.

Teaching Tips

For variety and a little more challenge, try Double Knee Boxing.

Double Knee Boxing.

In this contest, players try to touch both of their opponent's knees. As soon as a knee is touched, it must be covered for the remainder of the contest. For example, if Player 1 touches Player 2's left knee, Player 2 has to keep his left hand on that knee for the remainder of the contest. The first player to touch both of his opponent's knees wins.

SLAP JACK

Number of Participants	Grade Level	Activity Level	Playing Area
2 players per contest	4 and above	High	Anywhere

Recommended Equipment

⊙ None

Setup

Pair up students and have them stand opposite each other.

How to Play

At the signal to start, Player 1 extends his arms, palms facing up. Player 2 extends her arms, palms down, over Player 1's hands. Player 1, whose hands are on the bottom, attempts to slap the top of Player 2's hands before she can pull them away. When he misses, players reverse roles.

Safety Considerations

This contest is about speed—not to see how hard players can hit each other's hands. Discourage unnecessarily hard slaps.

Teaching Tips

While the challenge itself can be fun for students, those who get slapped often may get discouraged quickly. If certain students continually win, try pairing them up with other students who win often. You may also want to allow students to sit out if they do not want to participate in this contest.

STUCK UP

Number of Participants	Grade Level	Activity Level	Playing Area
5 to 10 players per team	8 and above	Low	Anywhere with a smooth wall

Recommended Equipment

- 1 roll of duct tape per team
- 1 chair per team
- 1 gymnastic mat per team
- 1 knife per team

Setup

Divide students into teams. (Try to assign at least 1 small student to each team.) Position the mats next to the wall and place a chair against the wall on each mat. Have the small students on each team stand on a chair and lean against the wall. Give each team 1 roll of duct tape and a knife.

How to Play

Players have 5 minutes to tape their teammate (the one on the chair) to the wall using duct tape. At the end of 5 minutes, they remove the chair. The team whose player stays up on the wall the longest wins.

Safety Considerations

Several precautions are advised in this activity.

- Caution students about knife safety and do not allow any shenanigans with the knife.
- Teammates should stand in front of the taped students in case they become unstuck and fall.
- To prevent the risk of strangulation should players start to slide down the wall, no tape is allowed above the shoulders.

- ◉ Instruct students to tape their teammates below their armpits.
- ◉ Have an extra knife handy in case a student needs to be cut down quickly.

Teaching Tips

Be sure to ask small students if they will agree to be taped up. If students are afraid of heights or are otherwise uncomfortable with the activity, do not force them.

Have a camera ready. The final result makes for a great picture.

THUMB WRESTLING

Number of Participants	Grade Level	Activity Level	Playing Area
2 students per contest*	4 and above	Low	Anywhere

Recommended Equipment

- ◉ None

Setup

Pair off students and have them stand or sit facing each other.

How to Play

Players assume the thumb-wrestling position: their right fingers hooked together, thumbs up. At the signal to start, players shinny off with their thumbs, hockey style (touching their index finger knuckle, then the tip of their index finger, then the knuckle) to the count of 3. Then they try to pin their opponent's thumb, without unhooking their fingers. The first player to pin the other's thumb wins.

Safety Considerations

Warn students not to yank their opponents' arms.

Teaching Tips

If you have left-handers in class, pair them up first.

For a real challenge and lots of laughs, have students thumb wrestle using their weak hand (left-handers wrestle with their right thumbs; right-handers wrestle with their left).

CHEST WRESTLING

Number of Participants	Grade Level	Activity Level	Playing Area
2 players per contest	8 and above	Medium	Anywhere

*It is recommended that players be of same gender.

Recommended Equipment

⊙ None

Setup

Demarcate 2 parallel lines approximately 5 yards (meters) apart. Pair off students and position them between these lines, facing each other, their hands joined behind their backs.

How to Play

At the start signal, players try to push their opponents backward, across the line they are facing. Players' chests must remain in contact throughout the match. If one player tries to avoid being pushed over the line by turning away, the other player wins. The first player to push an opponent across the line wins.

Safety Considerations

Do not allow students to make their opponents fall backward. To prevent crashes, make sure the lines are far enough away from walls.

Teaching Tips

For added fun, try this on a muddy field.

HIPPO WRESTLING

Number of Participants	Grade Level	Activity Level	Playing Area
2 students per contest	8 and above	Medium	Anywhere

Recommended Equipment

⊙ None

Setup

Demarcate 2 parallel lines approximately 5 yards (meters) apart. Pair up students and position them between these lines, standing backside-to-backside.

How to Play

At the start signal, players lean forward and try to push their opponents past their line. Players' backsides must remain in contact throughout the match. If players fall, turn to avoid going past their lines, or lose their balance and separate from their opponents, they automatically lose. The first player to push an opponent past the line wins.

Safety Considerations

Caution students about bumping or "checking" each other across the lines. Players must remain in contact throughout the match.

Teaching Tips

For some real fun, not to mention hippo realism, play this in the mud.

CHICKEN TOSS

Number of Participants	Grade Level	Activity Level	Playing Area
2 students per team	4 and above	Low	Anywhere, but preferably outside

Recommended Equipment

- 1 towel per team
- 1 rubber chicken (or other toy animal) per team
- 1 distance marker

Setup

Demarcate a throw-off line. Divide students into teams and have each team stand on the line, holding a towel with the rubber chicken on it.

How to Play

Players flip the towel to see how far they can make the chicken fly. Mark the longest toss with a flag or other distance marker. The team that tosses the chicken the farthest wins.

Safety Considerations

None

Teaching Tips

To increase team spirit and camaraderie among students, try the Chicken Catch.

Catch the Chicken

This variation requires 2 towels and 4 students per team. Position pairs of students 5 yards (meters) apart, each pair holding a towel. It will be easiest to determine the distance if you line up pairs of students together. One pair tosses the chicken to the other pair, who catches it in their towel. That pair then tosses the chicken back and the other pair catches it.

To increase the competition, have pairs of students move farther apart (2 or 3 feet) each round. The team that completes the longest toss and catch wins.

chapter 7

Individual
Challenges

● ● ● ● ● ● ● ●

LONGEST HANDSTAND

Number of Participants	Grade Level	Activity Level	Playing Area
Any number	8 and above	Medium	Any walled area

Recommended Equipment

⊙ 1 gymnastic mat per player

Setup

Place gymnastic mats next to a wall (or walls). Have each student stand on a mat.

How to Play

At the signal to start, players do a handstand against the wall. The player who maintains the position longest wins.

Safety Considerations

To prevent dizziness and subsequent falls or injuries, have students sit down when they come out of the handstand. You can also have a student (or students) available to help players roll safely out of the handstand when they get tired.

Teaching Tips

If students are able to hold a handstand longer than 2 minutes, have them hold the position without touching the wall. Or, have them do a push-up every 15 seconds while maintaining the handstand position. These variations will keep the activity moving and may help to relieve other students' restlessness.

WALL RUN

Number of Participants	Grade Level	Activity Level	Playing Area
Any number	4 and above	High	Any walled area

Recommended Equipment

- ⊙ 1 wrestling mat
- ⊙ Tape
- ⊙ 1 stopwatch

Setup

Place a wrestling mat on the floor against a wall. Place a piece of tape on the wall 1 yard (meter) in from both ends of the mat. The left tape is the start, the right tape is the finish. Line up students in the order they will compete and have the first student do a handstand at the start line.

How to Play

At the signal, players see how quickly they can "run" to the finish by walking with their hands on the ground and their feet against the wall. The fastest wall runner wins.

Safety Considerations

Be sure mats are tight against the wall before each student starts.

Teaching Tips

If you have enough wrestling mats, several students can run the wall at once. (You'll have to appoint a time-keeper for each student.) With enough mats, you can also have students wall-run for distance. The student who goes the farthest wins.

LONGEST HULA HOOP

Number of Participants	Grade Level	Activity Level	Playing Area
Any number	4 and above	High	Anywhere

Recommended Equipment

○ 1 hula hoop per player

Setup

Position students around the playing area so that they will not bump into one another while spinning their hula hoops. Give each student a hula hoop.

How to Play

At the signal to start, players spin their hoops around their waists. The one who keeps the hula hoop spinning the longest wins.

Safety Considerations

If holding this challenge outside on a hot day, be sure students get adequate fluids.

Teaching Tips

Be sure to allow enough time. Some students can go for hours. You may want to have a standby activity for students who are out of the running early.

Be fair. Make sure everyone starts at the same time.

LONGEST SPIT

Number of Participants	Grade Level	Activity Level	Playing Area
Any number	4 and above	Low	Grassy outside area

Recommended Equipment

- Sunflower seeds (or pumpkin seeds, black licorice, etc.)
- 1 distance marker (a coat hanger works well)

Setup

Ask for 2 volunteers to measure spitting distance. Designate a starting point and position the volunteers a few yards (meters) away. Line up the rest of the students in single file behind the starting point.

How to Play

This is essentially a spitting contest, but with sunflower seeds (or pumpkin seeds, black licorice, etc.) instead of saliva. One at a time, players advance to the starting point, put a sunflower seed in their mouths, and spit it out. Each player gets three tries.

Volunteers mark the longest spit with a marker, moving the marker only if that spit is exceeded by another player. The player who spits the farthest wins.

Safety Considerations

Caution students to stay clear of overspray, particularly the students measuring distance. Do not allow students to spit seeds at one another.

Teaching Tips

This activity can be messy. Be sure to have wash rags or towels available for students who dribble.

Have some fun with this activity by using targets or having students spit from different positions. For example, students could spin around and then spit, or they could spit backward between their legs.

STRING ROLL

Number of Participants	Grade Level	Activity Level	Playing Area
4 students per group	8 and above	Low	Anywhere

Recommended Equipment

- 1 string, 2 yards (meters) long, per player
- 1 pole per group

Setup

Divide students into groups and position each group around a pole to form an X (1 student at each direction: north, south, east, and west; these don't have to be exact). Tie 4 strings to each pole and have each student loop a string once around 2 of their fingers.

How to Play

At the signal to start, players roll the string on their fingers until their fingers touch the pole. The fastest student wins.

Safety Considerations

Warn students not to wrap the string so tightly around their fingers that it stops blood flow.

Teaching Tips

To make the game faster, have students wrap their strings around four of their fingers. The fastest student wins.

HAT DAY RACES

Number of Participants	Grade Level	Activity Level	Playing Area
Any number	4 and above	Low	Anywhere

Recommended Equipment

- ◉ 1 hat per student

Setup

Distribute hats to students.

How to Play

This game allows for many different challenges. For example, see which players can

- ◉ toss their hats and catch them on their heads the most times in 30 seconds,
- ◉ throw their hats onto their partner's head (standing 2 yards [meters] away) the most times in 30 seconds,
- ◉ throw their hats, flipping them once in the air, onto their partner's head (standing 2 yards [meters] away) the most times in 30 seconds,

- throw their hats the farthest, or
- throw their hats the highest (this might be somewhat difficult to measure).

Safety Considerations

Do not allow students to throw their hats at other students, particularly at their faces.

Teaching Tips

Challenge students to brainstorm other creative hat challenges. If you don't have enough hats for everyone in class, ask students to bring their own hats to the next class. (Be sure to provide some, in case students forget theirs.)

TAPE ROLL BOWLING

Number of Participants	Grade Level	Activity Level	Playing Area
Any number	4 and above	Low	Long hallway

Recommended Equipment

- 1 roll of tape
- 1 cardboard box

Setup

Place a cardboard box on its side in a hallway. Demarcate a start line approximately 15 yards (meters) away. Line up students, single file, behind this line.

How to Play

One at a time, players roll the tape, trying to get it into the cardboard box. When the roll of tape falls, the player rolls it again. If the tape hits a wall, the player rolls it from where it hit the wall. The player who rolls the tape into the box in the fewest rolls wins.

Safety Considerations

Make sure students do not throw the tape, particularly if there are doorways in the hallway.

Teaching Tips

For younger students, use wide rolls of tape. They're easier to hold onto and they are more stable.

WORLD'S STRONGEST PERSON

Number of Participants	Grade Level	Activity Level	Playing Area
Any number	8 and above	Low	Anywhere

Recommended Equipment

- 1 medicine ball
- 1 distance marker

Setup

Ask for a few volunteers to measure distance. Designate a throwing-off line. Line up the rest of the students, single file, behind this line. Give the first student the medicine ball.

How to Play

This is a distance challenge. Players may throw the ball any way they choose, but they must stay behind the line. Mark the longest distance. The player who throws the ball the farthest is the winner.

Safety Considerations

Have students stretch their arms before throwing the medicine ball.

Teaching Tips

To "level the playing field," use a balloon or have students throw the medicine ball with both hands.

HACKEY SAC DRIBBLE

Number of Participants	Grade Level	Activity Level	Playing Area
Any number	8 and above	Medium	Anywhere

Recommended Equipment

- 1 hackey sac per student

Setup

Position students around the playing area, at least 3 to 4 yards (meters) apart so that they can move around safely.

How to Play

At the signal to start, players toss the hackey sac in the air and then keep it up using their legs, thighs, shins, chest—anything but their arms and hands. When it hits the floor, that player is out. The last player "dribbling" the hackey sac wins.

Safety Considerations

Caution students to protect their faces, particularly their eyes.

Teaching Tips

If you don't have hackey sacs available, you can also use small beanbags. To promote camaraderie among students, try Team Hackey Sac Dribble.

Team Hackey Sac Dribble

Divide students into teams (2 or more students per team) and give 1 hackey sac (or beanbag) to each team. At the start signal, teammates keep the hackey sac up as long as they can. The last team dribbling wins.

CRAZY FOWL SHOTS

Number of Participants	Grade Level	Activity Level	Playing Area
Any number	4 and above	Low	Basketball court

Recommended Equipment

⊙ 1 rubber chicken

Setup

Have students stand in single file behind the free-throw line. Give the first student a rubber chicken.

How to Play

One at a time, each player takes 10 shots, trying to sink the chicken into the basket. The player who gets the most baskets wins. In the event of a tie, high-scoring players take an additional 10 shots.

Safety Considerations

Do not allow students to hit other players with the rubber chicken.

Teaching Tips

To make the challenge go faster, reduce the number of shots each student takes, or have each student shoot once and go through the line 10 times.

If you do not have a rubber chicken, any cloth, plastic, or rubber object will do—as long as it will fit in the basket. You can also use other items such as footballs, volleyballs, beanbags, and basketballs.

To "level the playing field" and make the game more entertaining to watch, require students to spin around before shooting or have them throw backward under their legs or over their heads.

SQUASH SERVE

Number of Participants	Grade Level	Activity Level	Playing Area
Any number	8 and above	Low	Squash court

Recommended Equipment

- 1 squash racquet per player
- 1 racquetball
- 1 gymnastic mat

Setup

Place a gymnastic mat in the back corner of a squash court. Have the student stand in the service box on the opposite side.

How to Play

The challenge is to serve a squash ball against the front wall and onto the gymnastic mat. Each player gets 10 tries. The one who gets the most serves on the mat wins.

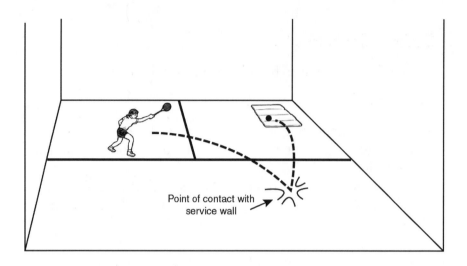

Point of contact with service wall

Safety Considerations

To encourage eye safety, students should wear goggles.

Teaching Tips

For younger students and inexperienced squash players, add another gymnastic mat for a larger target.

3-POINT SHOOTING

Number of Participants	Grade Level	Activity Level	Playing Area
Any number	8 and above	Low	Basketball court

Recommended Equipment

- ⊙ 5 basketballs
- ⊙ 1 stopwatch

Setup

Ask for 5 volunteers: 4 students stand near the basket to retrieve the balls and 1 stands beside the shooters to pass them the balls. Line up the rest of the students near the baseline.

How to Play

At the signal to start, 1 player steps up to the baseline and is given a ball. Each player has 75 seconds to take 25 shots: 5 shots from the left side of the baseline, 5 shots from halfway to the top of the arc, 5 shots from the top of the arc, 5 shots from 3/4 of the way around the arc, and 5 shots from the right side of the baseline. The first 4 shots of each 5-shot sequence are worth 1 point each; the last shot is worth 2 points. The highest possible score is 30 points. The player with the highest score is the winner.

Safety Considerations

To avoid crashes, and possibly injuries, among students retrieving the balls, assign them to positions in the court. Volunteers should retrieve only the balls that land in their area.

Teaching Tips

To maintain a rapid pace and reduce complaints of not having enough time to get in 25 shots, have the volunteer standing near the shooter pass a ball as soon as the shooter has thrown.

SPEEDO

Number of Participants	Grade Level	Activity Level	Playing Area
Any number	8 and above	High	Anywhere

Recommended Equipment

- 1 exercise bike with a speedometer

Setup

Set the tension on the exercise bike to accommodate all students. This tension should not be adjusted during the challenge.

How to Play

Players get 10 seconds to get the peddles turning and then an additional 5 seconds to accelerate to their fastest speed. Record the highest speed for each player. The player with the fastest speed wins.

Safety Considerations

Students who have heart problems should not participate in this activity.

Teaching Tips

Digital speedometers are the least subjective. If the only bike available has a speedometer dial, appoint 2 students to record the speeds.

LUNG CAPACITY

Number of Participants	Grade Level	Activity Level	Playing Area
Any number	4 and above	Low	Anywhere

Recommended Equipment

○ 1 balloon per player

Setup

Give each student a balloon.

How to Play

At the signal to start, players blow up their balloons. After 30 seconds, the player with the largest balloon wins.

Safety Considerations

Use nonallergenic balloons, and be sure students don't blow so hard or so quickly that they get dizzy.

Teaching Tips

Add some variety and fun to this activity. Have students run in place for 10 seconds before blowing up their balloons. Or have them sit down and blow once, then stand up and blow once, then spin around and blow once, then stand on one foot and blow once, and so on.

SKIP IT

Number of Participants	Grade Level	Activity Level	Playing Area
Any number	1 and above	High	Anywhere

Recommended Equipment

- 1 jump rope
- 1 stopwatch

Setup

Ask for 2 volunteers: 1 student will keep time and the other will count the number of skips. Line up the rest of the students around the time-keeper and the counter. Place the jump rope on the floor in front of the counter.

How to Play

The first player picks up the jump rope and gets ready. The time-keeper counts down from 3 and then starts the stopwatch: "3, 2, 1, start." Players skip rope for 20 seconds while the counter counts the number of skips. Jumps between rope revolutions do not count.

When the time-keeper calls out "Stop!" after 20 seconds, the player stops skipping and the counter records the number of skips. The player with the most skips in 20 seconds wins.

Safety Considerations

Students with heart problems should not participate in this challenge.

Teaching Tips

To involve more students at one time, try the Double Dutch.

Double Dutch

This is a team event in which 2 students move the rope and 2 students skip, or 2 players move 2 ropes (a true "Double Dutch") and 1 player skips. Divide students into teams of 3 and have them choose who will skip and who will move the rope(s). The team with the most skips in 20 seconds wins.

PING-PONG SERVE

Number of Participants	Grade Level	Activity Level	Playing Area
Any number	8 and above	Low	Ping pong table

Recommended Equipment

- 5 Ping-Pong balls
- 1 Ping-Pong paddle

Setup

Using masking (or other) tape, demarcate service-point areas on each side of the table (see illustration). The back triangle is worth 3 points, the front triangle (nearest the net) is worth 2 points, and the parallelogram between the triangles is worth 1 point.

Divide the class in half. Line up half of the students in single file at one side of the table and the other half at the other side.

How to Play

Players take turns serving 5 balls each, trying to get the most points. (Players on the other side of the table should catch the balls after they bounce.) Keep track of each player's score. After everyone has served, the player with the highest score wins.

Safety Considerations

Warn students to be on the lookout for flying Ping-Pong balls.

Teaching Tips

Make this activity more challenging by adjusting the scoring: The back triangle is worth 2 points, the front triangle (nearest the net) is worth 1 points, and the parallelogram between the triangles is worth 0 points.

- You could also make this a race against time. Students get 20 seconds, serving as many balls as they can in that time, to score as many points as they can.

HOLE-IN-ONE

Number of Participants	Grade Level	Activity Level	Playing Area
Any number	4 and above	Low	Carpeted surface

Recommended Equipment

- 1 golf ball
- 1 putter
- 1 putting target

Setup

Set up a putting target (plastic putting holes are inexpensive and work well for this game). Demarcate the putting line approximately 5 yards (meters) from the target and line up students behind the line.

How to Play

One at a time, players get five putts to see how many holes-in-one they can get. Keep track of each player's score. After everyone has putted, the player with the most holes-in-one wins.

Safety Considerations

To prevent students from getting hit, and other injuries, make sure that students use the putter as a putter—not as an iron or wood, or sword, or dagger, and so on.

Teaching Tips

Make the challenge easier by putting the target closer to the putting line. Add variety and more challenge by having students putt from their weak sides, use the putter like a pool cue (lying down to shoot), or not use the putter but instead kick the ball into the hole.

You may want to ask for volunteers to retrieve the balls, depending on the putting skill of your students.

WATER GUZZLE

Number of Participants	Grade Level	Activity Level	Playing Area
Any number	4 and above	Low	Near a water fountain

Recommended Equipment

- ⊙ 1 stopwatch
- ⊙ 1 cup per participant

Setup

Line up students near the water fountain. Give each student a cup.

How to Play

At the signal to start, one at a time, players go to the drinking fountain, fill their cups with water, and guzzle it down. When their cups are empty, players place them upside-down on top of their heads and the clock is stopped. The fastest guzzler is the winner.

Safety Considerations

Warn students not to guzzle so fast that they choke. Do not allow water fights and other shenanigans around the water fountain.

Teaching Tips

Make this a team relay by dividing students into teams of 4 or more. Each team guzzles as many cupfuls as they can within 20 seconds. The team with the most empty cups placed upside-down on their heads wins. (Cups that fall on the floor do not count, but cup stacking is allowed.)

BALLOON KICK

Number of Participants	Grade Level	Activity Level	Playing Area
Any number	4 and above	Low	Anywhere

Recommended Equipment

- 1 balloon
- 1 distance marker

Setup

Demarcate a starting line and line up students, single file, behind this line. Place a balloon on the line.

How to Play

One at a time, players kick the balloon as far as they can. The longest kick is marked (measure first bounce or farthest roll). The player who kicks the balloon the farthest wins.

Safety Considerations

Use nonallergenic balloons and do not allow students to pop the balloons near each other's ears.

Teaching Tips

To speed up the game, have several students kick balloons at once. Divide students into groups and align them at the starting line. The first player in each line kicks at the same time.

part II

Modifying Traditional Games

chapter 8

Baseball Games

• • • • • • • •

3-PITCH BASEBALL

Number of Participants	Grade Level	Activity Level	Playing Area
2 teams of 10 students	6 and above	Medium	Baseball diamond

Recommended Equipment

- 4 bases
- 3 bats (different sizes)
- 1 baseball
- 10 baseball gloves

Setup

Divide students into teams and devise a batting order for each team. Position the bases 20 yards (meters) apart. Draw a commitment line between third base and home plate, 5 yards (meters) from third base.

Line up the offense behind the backstop, according to batting order, with the last student to bat on the pitching mound. (When it is the pitcher's turn to bat, the team selects another pitcher.)

Position the defense: 1 catcher; players on first, second, and third; 1 shortstop between second and third; and 5 outfielders.

How to Play

The game goes 40 minutes (or longer or shorter, depending on class time). Players hit the ball and run the bases, just like regular baseball (but see the following Rules). When the offense gets 3 outs, the other team bats. The team with the most runs at the end of the game wins.

Rules

- Each batter gets 3 pitches (3 strikes) only. Misses and fouls count as strikes. No balls are counted.
- No bunting is allowed. If the ball does not pass the diagonal between first and third, it's a strike.
- A foul ball is an automatic out. A ball will be judged foul if it either lands outside the baseline along first base or third base or it lands infield and then goes out of bounds before it passes first or third base.
- The infield fly rule is in effect. With less than 2 outs and runners on first and second or bases loaded, the batter is automatically out on an infield fly.
- Caught balls are automatic outs. Runners cannot advance on a caught fly.
- Pitchers cannot interfere with defensive play. If a pitcher contacts the ball after a hit, the batter is out and all runners return to their bases.
- No lead-offs or steals are allowed. The ball must be hit before runners leave a base. (If a player is caught leading off, it's an automatic out.)
- Runners may advance 1 base on overthrows that end up in foul territory.
- Sliding into bases is not permitted.
- Once runners pass the commitment line, they must continue to home plate.

⊙ To get a runner out, the catcher must catch the ball and touch home plate before the runner crosses the plate. The runner does not need to tag the runner coming home.

Safety Considerations

If available, use a safety base on first. This base is twice as wide as regular bases, which enables the first-base player to keep a foot on the bag without tripping the runner. Require catchers and pitchers to wear face masks, and do not allow students to wear cleats.

Teaching Tips

Since no umpire is required to call strikes and balls, you can stand off to the side to call the game and keep score.

To accommodate a range of batting skills among students, have bats of different sizes and weights available. (Beginners do better with lighter bats.)

To be fair, make sure both teams get equal times at bat. Either limit the game to 5 innings or, 10 minutes before the end of class, call out "Ten minutes!" to let students know that the starting defense will get a last turn at bat.

In the case of a tie, use the score at the end of the previous inning.

EVERYONE HITS

Number of Participants	Grade Level	Activity Level	Playing Area
2 teams of 10 players	6 and above	Medium	Baseball diamond

Recommended Equipment

⊙ 4 bases

⊙ 3 bats (different sizes)

⊙ 1 baseball

⊙ 10 baseball gloves

Setup

Divide students into teams and devise a batting order for each team. Position bases 20 yards (meters) apart. Draw a commitment line between third base and home plate, 5 yards (meters) from third base.

Line up the offense behind the backstop, according to batting order, with the last student to bat on the pitching mound. (When it is the pitcher's turn to bat, the team selects another pitcher.) Position the defense: 1 catcher; players on first, second, and third, 1 shortstop between second and third; and 5 outfielders.

How to Play

The game is like 3-Pitch Baseball (see page 139), except each player gets to bat once and only 4 innings are played. When all 10 players have batted, the teams switch—regardless of how many are out. When the last batter is up, the pitcher calls "Last batter!" After the ball is hit, the defense throws home to stop runners from scoring. The team with the most runs at the end of 4 innings wins.

Safety Considerations

If available, use a safety base on first. This base is twice as wide as regular bases, which enables the first-base player to keep a foot on the bag without tripping the runner. Require catchers and pitchers to wear face masks, and do not allow students to wear cleats.

Teaching Tips

Since no umpire is required to call strikes and balls, you can stand off to the side to call the game and keep score.

To accommodate a range of batting skills among students, have bats of different sizes and weights available. (Beginners do better with lighter bats.)

HAND BASEBALL

Number of Participants	Grade Level	Activity Level	Playing Area
2 teams of 10 students	6 and above	Medium	Baseball diamond

Recommended Equipment

- ⊙ 4 bases
- ⊙ 1 playground ball (a soft ball, 4 inches in diameter)

Setup

Divide students into teams and devise a batting order for each team. Position bases as in regular baseball, but only 15 yards (meters) apart. Draw a commitment line between third base and home plate, 5 yards (meters) from third base.

Line up the offense behind the backstop, according to batting order, with the last student to bat on the pitching mound in the center of the diamond. (When it is the pitcher's turn to bat, the team selects another pitcher.) Position the defense: 1 catcher; players on first, second, and third, 1 shortstop between second and third; and 5 outfielders. Since the ball will not travel as far, defense should play closer to homeplate.

How to Play

This game is a lot like 3-Pitch Baseball (see page 139) but with two major exceptions.

1. No bat or gloves are used. Players bat and catch the ball with their hands.

2. Because it is more difficult to hit long distances without using a bat, the distance between bases is reduced (see Setup earlier) to allow players enough time to run the bases.

At the end of 4 innings, the team with the most runs wins.

Safety Considerations

Batting with the hand puts stress on the elbows, so this game should not be played too often

Teaching Tips

This game can also be played indoors. All walls are in play. Add some challenge by using soft balls of different sizes, for example, a tennis or beach ball.

KICK BASEBALL

Number of Participants	Grade Level	Activity Level	Playing Area
2 teams of 10 players	4 and above	Medium	Baseball diamond

Recommended Equipment

- 4 bases
- 1 soccer (or playground) ball

Setup

Divide students into teams and devise a kicking order for each team. Position bases 20 yards (meters) apart. Draw a commitment line between third base and home plate, 5 yards (meters) from third base.

Line up the offense behind the backstop, according to kicking order, with the last student to kick on the pitching mound. (When it is the pitcher's turn to kick, the team selects another pitcher.) Position the defense: 1 catcher; players on first, second, and third, 1 shortstop between second and third; and 5 outfielders.

How to Play

The rules of 3-Pitch Baseball (see page 139) apply but with one major exception: the pitcher rolls the ball to the kicker, who kicks the ball into play. At the end of 4 innings, the team with the most runs wins.

Safety Considerations

If available, use a safety base on first. This base is twice as wide as regular bases, which enables the first-base player to keep a foot on the bag without tripping the runner.

Teaching Tips

Add some challenge, and lots of smiles and laughter, by trying Bladder Kickball.

Bladder Kickball

In this variation, the bladder of a soccer ball is used instead of a soccer ball. In addition, the bladder ball is placed on home plate and kicked into play; no pitcher is used. A bladder ball greatly reduces kicking distance and, with its sporadic and unpredictable movement, adds a lot of fun to the game. Because it is difficult to kick a bladder very far, it may be a good idea to reduce the distance between bases to 15 yards (meters). This game can also be played indoors.

SPEED BASEBALL

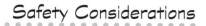

Number of Participants	Grade Level	Activity Level	Playing Area
2 teams of 10 students	6 and above	Medium	Baseball diamond

Recommended Equipment

- 4 bases
- 3 bats (different sizes)
- 1 baseball
- 10 baseball gloves

Setup

Divide students into teams and devise a batting order for each team. Position bases 20 yards (meters) apart. Draw a commitment line between third base and home plate, 5 yards (meters) from third base.

Line up the offense behind the backstop, according to batting order, with the last student to bat on the pitching mound. (When it is the pitcher's turn to bat, the team selects another pitcher.) Position the defense: 1 catcher; players on first, second, and third, 1 shortstop between second and third; and 5 outfielders.

How to Play

This game is played like 3-Pitch Baseball (see page 139) but with one exception: as soon as the pitcher and batter are ready, they can start. This exception, while minor, makes for a faster game and higher scoring early in each team's batting order. Defense and offense try to switch places quickly—in particular, the pitcher and first batter on the offense, and the outfielders and first-base player on the defense. At the end of 5 innings, the team with the most runs wins.

Safety Considerations

This game presents a considerable safety risk because a student who is not ready may get hit by a bat or ball. To minimize this risk and warn students to pay attention—not to mention hurrying students to their positions—call out "Play ball!" when it is safe to proceed.

Teaching Tips

The exception in this game—offensive players being able to start when they are ready—can be applied to the other games in this chapter as well. In particular, try it with Hand Baseball (page 143) and Kick Baseball (page 144.

BEAT THE BALL HOME

Number of Participants	Grade Level	Activity Level	Playing Area
2 teams of 10 players	4 and above	Medium	Baseball diamond

Recommended Equipment

- 4 bases
- 3 bats (different sizes)
- 1 baseball
- 10 baseball gloves

Setup

Divide students into teams and devise a batting order for each team. Position bases 20 yards (meters) apart. Draw a commitment line between third base and home plate, 5 yards (meters) from third base.

Line up the offense behind the backstop, according to batting order, with the last student to bat on the pitching mound. (When it is the pitcher's turn to bat, the team selects another pitcher.) Position the defense: 1 catcher; players on first, second, and third, 1 shortstop between second and third; and 5 outfielders.

How to Play

Batters must, after a fair hit, run all the bases before the base players, after catching or fielding the hit, throw the ball from first base to second base to third base to home plate. If the ball reaches home plate before the runner, the runner is out. If the runner reaches home plate before the ball, the runner gets a run. Many of the rules of 3-Pitch Baseball (see page 139) apply to this game.

Rules

- Each batter gets 3 pitches (3 strikes) only. Misses and fouls count as strikes. No balls are counted.
- No bunting is allowed. If the ball does not pass the diagonal between first and third, it's a strike.
- A foul ball is an automatic out. A ball will be judged foul if it either lands outside the baseline along first base or third base or it lands infield and then goes out of bounds before it passes first or third base.
- Caught fly balls are automatic outs.
- Pitchers cannot interfere with defensive play. If a pitcher contacts the ball after a hit, the batter is out.

At the end of 4 innings, the team with the most runs wins.

Safety Considerations

To reduce the risk of head injuries, base players and batters (runners) should wear helmets. For younger students, use a softball or a playground ball.

Teaching Tips

The distance between bases may need to be shortened from 20 yards (meters) to 10 or 15 yards (meters) to enable runners to get around the bases and score a run.

This game could also be applied to Everyone Hits (page 141) and Speed Baseball (page 145).

CROSS-OUT BASEBALL

Number of Participants	Grade Level	Activity Level	Playing Area
2 teams of 10 players	6 and above	Medium	Baseball diamond

Recommended Equipment

- 4 bases
- 3 bats (different sizes)
- 1 baseball
- 10 baseball gloves

Setup

Divide students into teams and devise a batting order for each team. Position bases 20 yards (meters) apart, and line up the offense behind the backstop, according to batting order, with the last student to bat on the pitching mound. (When it is the pitcher's turn to bat, the team selects another pitcher.) Position the defense: 1 catcher; players on first, second, and third, 1 shortstop between second and third; and 5 outfielders.

How to Play

This game is played like 3-Pitch Baseball (see page 139) but with two exceptions.

1. Runners are out if a defensive player (outfielder or base player) with the ball runs between them and the base they are running toward. Defensive players may also throw the ball at a base player, who then stands between the runner and the base.
2. All bases have an invisible commitment line. Once a runner has left the base, there is no turning back.

After 4 innings, the team with the most runs wins.

Safety Considerations

Instruct runners to be careful not to run into their teammates.

Teaching Tips

The distance between bases can be lengthened from 20 to 25 yards (meters) to give defensive players a fair chance at intercepting the runner's path.

Add some challenge by using soft balls of different sizes, for example, a tennis or beach ball.

BASES LOADED

Number of Participants	Grade Level	Activity Level	Playing Area
2 teams of 10 players	6 and above	Medium	Baseball diamond

Recommended Equipment

- 4 bases
- 3 bats (different sizes)
- 1 baseball
- 10 baseball gloves

Setup

Divide students into teams and devise a batting order for each team. Position bases 20 yards (meters) apart. Draw a commitment line between third base and home plate, 5 yards (meters) from third base.

Line up the offense behind the backstop, according to batting order, with the last student to bat on the pitching mound. (When it is the pitcher's turn to bat, the team selects another pitcher.) Position the defense: 1 catcher; players on first, second, and third, 1 shortstop between second and third; and 5 outfielders.

How to Play

This game is played like 3-Pitch Baseball (see page 139), except base runners do not have to advance and there are no forced outs. As many runners can be on 1 base as can touch the bag at a time, but if they are not touching the base, a base player can tag them out. After 4 innings, the team with the most runs wins.

Safety Considerations

Instruct runners to be careful not to run into their teammates.

Teaching Tips

Use the rules of this game to add some variety to other games in this chapter. (Hand Baseball [page 143] and Kick Baseball [page 144] would work well.)

FRISBEE BASEBALL

Number of Participants	Grade Level	Activity Level	Playing Area
2 teams of 10 students	4 and above	Medium	Baseball diamond

Recommended Equipment

- 4 bases
- 1 Frisbee

Setup

Divide students into teams and devise a batting order for each team. Position bases 20 yards (meters) apart, and line up the offense behind the backstop, according to batting order. Position the defense: 1 catcher; players on first, second, and third, 1 short-stop between second and third; and 5 outfielders.

How to Play

This game is like 3-Pitch Baseball (see page 139), except batters throw a Frisbee rather than hit a ball and, thus, there is no pitcher.

When up to bat, each batter throws the Frisbee once. Like 3-Pitch Baseball,

- the Frisbee must fly past the diagonal between first and third bases (no "bunting"),
- if a runner is caught leading off, it's an automatic out,
- if the Frisbee lands out of bounds, it's an automatic out,
- the infield fly rule is in effect,
- caught Frisbees are automatic outs,
- runners may advance 1 base on overthrows that end up in the foul territory,
- sliding into bases is not permitted, and
- to get a runner out, the catcher must catch the Frisbee and touch home plate before the runner crosses the plate.

Unlike 3-Pitch Baseball,

- a throw out of bounds is an automatic out and
- runners cannot run until the Frisbee is thrown.

At the end of 4 innings, the team with the most runs wins.

Safety Considerations

To reduce the risk of head injuries, base runners should wear helmets.

Teaching Tips

Frisbees can be used in other games in this chapter, for example, Cross-Out Baseball (page 148) and Bases Loaded Baseball (page 150).

1800's BASEBALL

Number of Participants	Grade Level	Activity Level	Playing Area
2 teams of 10 students	6 and above	Medium	Baseball diamond

Recommended Equipment

- 4 bases
- 3 wooden bats (different sizes)
- 1 soft (cloth) ball

Setup

Divide students into teams and devise a batting order for each team. Position the bases 30 yards (meters) apart.

Line up the offense behind the backstop, according to batting order. Position the defense: 1 catcher; 1 pitcher; players on first, second, and third; 1 shortstop between second and third; and 4 outfielders.

How to Play

A gentile variation of baseball, 1800s Baseball is like old-fashioned baseball in that everyone is polite and the rules are simple.

Rules

- Pitchers ask batters where they want the ball and try to pitch to that spot.
- Batters get 3 actual (swing and miss) strikes, and 3 strikes make 1 out.
- Each team gets 3 outs.
- No stealing bases—that would not be very gentlemanly!
- A caught fly ball is any ball caught in the air or after 1 bounce off the ground (in the field or in foul territory).

- No sliding into base.
- Runners cannot be tagged out when they are not on base.

The team that scores the most runs in 9 innings wins.

Safety Considerations

Because a soft ball is used, risk of head injury is minimal. If you shoot for real authenticity and play on an open field (or pasture or other bumpy playing surface), students should be careful that they don't sprain an ankle while running the bases.

Teaching Tips

For a list of the early rules of baseball, as well as tips and information on umpiring youth baseball, check out PVLL's (Prescott Valley [Arizona] Little League Umpires) Web site: http://www.eteamz.com/pvazumpire/umphistory/.

SCOOTER BASEBALL

Number of Participants	Grade Level	Activity Level	Playing Area
2 teams of 10 players	4 and above	Medium	Gymnasium

Recommended Equipment

- 4 bases
- 1 plastic bat
- 1 plastic baseball (whiffle ball)
- 15 scooters

Setup

Divide students into teams and devise a batting order for each team. Position the bases 10 yards (meters) apart.

Line up the offense behind the backstop, according to batting order, with the last student to bat on the pitching mound. (When

it is the pitcher's turn to bat, the team selects another pitcher.)
Position the defense: 1 catcher; players on first, second, and third,
1 shortstop between second and third; and 5 outfielders.

How to Play

The rules of 3-Pitch Baseball (see page 139) apply with one major exception: all players throw, bat, and move about while seated on scooters. In addition, because this game is played indoors, all walls are in play.

At the end of 4 innings, the team with the most runs wins.

Safety Considerations

Be careful that students do not run over one another's fingers.

Teaching Tips

Several of the games in this chapter can be played inside on scooters as well, in particular: Hand Baseball (page 143) and Bases Loaded (page 150).

chapter 9

Basketball Games

● ● ● ● ● ● ● ●

RECREATIONAL BASKETBALL

Number of Participants	Grade Level	Activity Level	Playing Area
2 teams of 5 to 12 players*	4 and above	High	Basketball court

*if more than 5 players make substitutions

Recommended Equipment

- 1 basketball per game
- 1 jersey (or pinny) per player, one color for each team

Setup

Divide students into teams and distribute the jerseys to each team. Have each team select 5 players to start and assign their positions (2 forwards, 2 defense, and 1 center).

How to Play

Like basketball, the purpose of this game is to get as many baskets as possible. Field shots (baskets scored in regular play) are worth 2 points.

The game consists of two 15-minute halves, but halves can be shortened if necessary. The clock stops during time-outs and at breaks in the action (i.e., foul shots, putting the ball into play after it goes out of bounds, etc.) during the last minute of the second half—if there is a spread of 15 points or less. If the spread is more than 15 points, it is better to finish the game expeditiously.

The game starts with the starting lineup from each team on the court, team centers at the centerline. The official throws the basketball in the air and the centers jump for it, trying to hit the ball to a teammate on its way down. The other 8 players distribute themselves just outside the jump-ball circle at center court.

Rules

1. Each team can call 2 20-second time-outs per game.

2. The other team throws the ball to a teammate from the sideline when

   ⊚ offensive fouls are called (when offensive players run into defensive players who are not moving, or when offensive players are moving while blocking defensive players),

   ⊚ offensive players stay in the key longer than 3 seconds; dribble the ball, stop, and then dribble the ball again; or travel (walk or run the ball without dribbling), or

   ⊚ defensive fouls are called (when a defensive player touches an offensive player with the ball, or when a defensive player holds an offensive player).

3. Teams have 10 seconds to get the ball over center. Once the ball is over center, a team cannot return over center with the ball again. (This is called "over-and-back," and the other team gets the ball at the sideline at center court.)

4. Two foul shots (worth 1 point each) are awarded if a defensive foul occurs when an offensive player is taking a shot. The player fouled stands at the free-throw line while defensive and offensive players alternate themselves around the

key. If the second free throw goes into the basket, the defensive team tosses the ball in from behind their end line. Otherwise, both teams try to gain possession of the ball by rebounding.

5. Technical fouls are called when players yell at the referee or otherwise misbehave (tripping, shoving, and so on). The other team gets 1 free throw and then brings the ball into play from the sideline at center court.

6. Players who get 5 fouls (offensive and defensive) or 2 technical fouls are ejected from the game.

To ensure equal playing time, players are substituted at every stop in the action. At the end of the game, the team with the most points wins.

Safety Considerations

Whenever you see rough play, call a technical foul.

Teaching Tips

You might want to assign positions to all players for efficient substitutions. For example, designate 4 forwards, 3 centers, and 4 defense on each team. Some coaches and instructors stop play every few minutes for complete line changes.

If you have more than 24 students in class, try Half-Court Basketball. To "level the playing field," try Non-Dominant Basketball. To speed up the game, try Foul-Points Basketball.

Half-Court Basketball

This game is just like Recreational Basketball, except it is played using only half of the court (up to 48 students can play). The rules are the same, with one exception. After one team gets a basket, the other team gets the ball at half court. The other team also gets the ball at half court on a defensive rebound or turnover.

Non-Dominant Basketball

Students dribble and shoot with their non-dominant hands.

Foul-Points Basketball

Foul shooting can take up a fair amount of time. To get around this, simply award automatic foul points. A defensive foul is worth 2 points and the offensive team gets the ball. A technical foul is worth 1 point and the other team gets the ball. Offensive fouls are not worth points, but the defensive team gets the ball.

CO-ED BASKETBALL

Number of Participants	Grade Level	Activity Level	Playing Area
2 teams of 5 to 12 players	4 and above	High	Basketball court

Recommended Equipment

- ⊙ 1 basketball
- ⊙ 1 jersey (or pinny) per player, one color for each team

Setup

Divide students into teams and distribute the jerseys to each team. Have each team select 5 players to start and assign their positions (2 forwards, 2 defense, and 1 center).

How to Play

This is the same as Recreational Basketball (see page 157) but is specifically designed to involve females in the game. The rules of Recreational Basketball apply, with three exceptions.

1. Team gender must be balanced. That is, at least 4 females (2 on each team) must be on the court at all times.

2. Males are not allowed in the key at any time. If a male on offense goes into the key, the other team gets the ball. If a male on defense goes into the key, the other team gets 2 fouls shots.

3. Baskets scored by females count double: field shots are worth 4 points and foul shots are worth 2 points.

Safety Considerations

When you see rough or overly physical play, call a technical foul.

Teaching Tips

You could also require male players to dribble and shoot with their nondominant hands while females play with their dominant hands.

3-ON-3 BASKETBALL

Number of Participants	Grade Level	Activity Level	Playing Area
3-5 per team*	4 and above	High	Basketball court

*if more than 3 players, make substitutions

Recommended Equipment

- ◉ 1 basketball
- ◉ 1 jersey (or pinny) per player, one color for each team

Setup

Divide students into teams and distribute the jerseys to each team. Have each team select 3 players to start and assign their positions (1 forward, 1 defense, and 1 center). Flip a coin to see which team starts with the ball.

How to Play

As in Recreational Basketball (see page 157), teams try to outscore each other (each field shot is worth 2 points; foul shots are worth 1 point). At the end of the game, the team with the most points wins.

Unlike Recreational Basketball, players call their own fouls and games are played half-court, which means the following rule variations:

⊙ After a basket is scored, the other team gets the ball at the center line.

⊙ When the defensive team gets a rebound or steals the ball from the offensive team, they must take the ball outside the 3-point line before trying to score.

Safety Considerations

Because players call their own fouls, caution students that rough play often leads to violence. If students cannot referee themselves, you may have to step in and eject a player.

Teaching Tips

This game can also be played with Coed Basketball rules (see page 160). Each team would be required to have at least 1 female and 1 male on the court at all times.

SCOOTER BASKETBALL

Number of Participants	Grade Level	Activity Level	Playing Area
2 teams of 5 to 12 players	4 and above	High	Basketball court

Recommended Equipment

- 1 basketball
- 1 jersey (or pinny) per player, one color for each team
- 1 scooter per player

Setup

Divide students into teams, and distribute the jerseys and scooters to each team. Have each team select 5 players to start and assign their positions (2 forwards, 2 defense, and 1 center). Have players get into position, seated on scooters, on the court and flip a coin to determine which team will start with the ball.

How to Play

As in Recreational Basketball (see page 157), teams try to outscore each other (each field shot is worth 2 points; foul shots are worth 1 point). At the end of the game, the team with the most points wins.

The starting team throws the ball in from the sideline at center court. From there, Recreational Basketball rules apply, with one addition: if players run into each other or impede other players' scooters in any way, fouls are called (offensive, defensive, or technical, depending on who initiated the foul). Player substitutions can only happen at a stoppage in play.

Safety Considerations

Warn students to be careful about running over other players (fingers, feet, and so on) during the action. Also, be on the lookout for deliberate collisions and eject "rough riders" from the game.

Teaching Tips

For a large class, this game could be played on a half-court (see Half-Court Basketball on page 159). Likewise, the rules of Nondominant Basketball (page 159) and Foul-Points Basketball (page 159) can be applied to "level the playing field" and speed up the game.

BOUNCERS

Number of Participants	Grade Level	Activity Level	Playing Area
2 to 30 students	4 and above	Medium	Basketball court

Recommended Equipment

⊙ 1 basketball per player

Setup

Have students stand inside the half-court (or smaller court area if you have less than 20 students). Give each player a basketball.

How to Play

The object of the game is to be the last player bouncing a basketball. At the signal to start, players dribble a basketball within the court boundaries while trying to knock other players' balls away (using their free hands).

If players (their feet, hands, arms, and so on) or the ball they are bouncing go outside the boundaries, they are out of the game. If players lose their balls (when other players try to knock them away), they are out of the game.

Once players are out of the game, they must retrieve their balls and stand on the sidelines. Out players may not enter the court but may reach in and try to knock balls away from players still in the game. (Obviously, players still in the game will want to stay away from the sides.) The last player left bouncing a ball is the winner.

Safety Considerations

Warn students to avoid collisions with other players by looking out for one another.

Teaching Tips

To speed up the game, reduce the size of the court. For example, try the game with 30 students in a badminton court.

MONSTER BASKETBALL

Number of Participants	Grade Level	Activity Level	Playing Area
2 teams of 5 to 10 players	8 and above	High	Basketball court

Recommended Equipment

- 1 large ball (at least 1 yard [meter] in diameter)
- 1 jersey (or pinny) per player, one color for each team

Setup

Divide students into teams and distribute team jerseys. Position teams on their own half of the court.

How to Play

This game is like Recreational Basketball (see page 157), except that all players may be on the court at one time and players hit any part of the backboard to score (each contact is worth 1 point).

The game starts with an official throwing the ball up in the air. Any players can jump for it. Teams advance toward the basket by kicking or throwing the ball, but they may not carry it and move at the same time. When a point is scored, the other team gets to start the ball at the centerline.

If the ball goes out of bounds, play stops and a player from the other team throws it in from the sideline. In the event of deliberate grabbing, shoving, or tackling, the other team gets a free throw (1 point for hitting the backboard).

Safety Considerations

Some large balls can be heavy, especially for smaller players. To avoid wrist injuries, warn students not to punch or fling the ball with their hands.

Teaching Tips

For some variety, not to mention lots of fun, try Noodle Basketball.

Noodle Basketball

Instead of a large ball, this game uses balloons. Players advance the balloons down the court and shoot them toward the backboard using foam tubes. Used to insulate outdoor or exposed water pipes, these tubes are readily available at hardware stores. For the best control, cut the tubes to lengths of no more than 1 yard (meter).

chapter 10

Football Games

FLAG FOOTBALL

Number of Participants	Grade Level	Activity Level	Playing Area
2 teams of 5 to 7 players	6 and above	Medium	Football field

Recommended Equipment

- 1 football
- 1 set of flags per player
- 1 jersey (or pinny) per player, one color for each team

Setup

Using lime divide the field into fourths (each a 25-yard [meter] interval) with an end zone at either end, as shown in the illustration. Divide students into teams and distribute the jerseys. Have each team select a quarterback (or students can take turns between plays).

Flip a coin to see who will kick off. The team that wins the coin toss (offense) lines up behind their end zone line for the kick-off. The other team (defense) scatters behind centerfield to receive the kick-off.

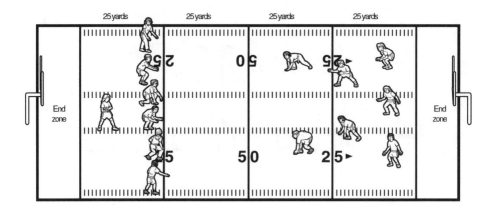

How to Play

The object is to get the ball into the opponent's end zone (a touchdown, worth 7 points). The game consists of 2 halves, each 15 to 20 minutes. At the last minute of each half, call out "One minute remaining!" Then stop the clock between plays for the rest of the half. Allow a 2-minute break at halftime.

This game is played like regular football with the following exceptions.

1. Players wear 2 flags on either side of their waist. When a flag is removed from a ball carrier, play stops at that spot.

2. The game starts (and is restarted after a touchdown) with a kick-off, taken from the defensive team's 25-yard line with either a place kick (ball standing on end on the ground or a kicking tee) or a punt. The ball must travel at least 25 yards (1 field interval on a kick-off). If it doesn't, the receiving (offensive) team may either catch the ball and run with it or take possession where the ball lands.

3. The ball is alive after a kick-off, which means that anyone from either team can pick up the ball. The kicking team has to wait till the ball passes the 50 yard line

4. Like football, from the line of scrimmage (where the ball is placed to start a play), the offense has 4 downs to advance the ball into the next zone (25-yard interval). If successful, the team gets 4 more downs. If unsuccessful, the defense takes the ball and becomes the offense.

5. Quarterbacks get 5 seconds to initiate a play without obstruction. (The referee counts it out: "1, steamboat, 2, steamboat," and so on.) The defense may not rush across the line of scrimmage and no running plays may occur during this time. After the steamboat count, the defense may rush the quarterback and the quarterback (or another player) may run the ball.

6. A 5-yard penalty is awarded for taking more than 10 seconds in a huddle and offsides (crossing the line of scrimmage before the ball is given to the quarterback).

7. Any player may catch the ball, but players are stopped where the ball carriers flags are removed.

8. A 10-yard penalty and an automatic first down are awarded (at point of infraction) for offensive interference (contacting receivers when they are trying to catch the ball).

9. Ball carriers may not defend their flags by using their hands, spinning, or otherwise preventing the defense from snagging their flags.

10. If offensive players block, tackle, shove, trip, push, or use other rough physical contact with other players, they lose that down and the ball is returned to the original line of scrimmage.

11. Except in the opening kick-off, the ball is automatically dead when it touches the ground. Play resumes at the line of scrimmage or where that ball was fumbled, whichever is furthest down field.

12. On the fourth down, the offense may punt the ball or try for a first down. If they punt and the ball goes through the back of the end zone, a player's flag is removed in their end zone, the defense takes possession of the ball (becoming the offense) 10-yards in front of their end zone. Players receiving a punt must be given 5 yards to receive the kick before going after their flags.

13. If defensive players grab or block ball carriers or use rough play, the offense gets a 10-yard bonus from the point of infraction or where the ball was grounded, whichever is farthest downfield, plus an automatic first down.

14. A half cannot end on a kick-off or on a play in which there was a defensive penalty; players will have to play 1 more down.

Safety Considerations

To reduce risk of injury, be sure to enforce rules against violent behavior.

Teaching Tips

Try switching from U.S. rules to Canadian football rules, which use 3 downs instead of 4.

To add a bit of contact to the game, which often means more fun, try Touch Football. For some variety, try Frisbee Football.

Touch Football

Rather than snatching flags, players need only touch the ball carrier with one hand below the waist or both hands anywhere. This is a little more elusive, however, because players often disagree about whether or not the ball carrier was actually tagged.

Frisbee Football

In this game, players follow the same rules of Flag Football but use a Frisbee instead of a football.

INCH FOOTBALL

Number of Participants	Grade Level	Activity Level	Playing Area
2 teams of 4 to 7 players	6 and above	Medium	Gymnasium, on wrestling mats

Recommended Equipment

- 1 football
- 1 set of flags per player
- 1 jersey (or pinny) per player, one color for each team
- Tape

Setup

Tape 1-yard (meter) lines across the mat at both ends to designate each team's end zone. Divide students into teams and distribute the jerseys. Have each team select a quarterback (or students can take turns between plays).

Flip a coin to see who will kick off. The team that wins the coin toss (offense) begins on their end zone line.

How to Play

This game is just like Flag Football (see page 167), except the field is much smaller (a wrestling mat), players remain on their knees throughout the game, and each team has 4 downs to score a touchdown.

Safety Considerations

Make sure that students stay on the mat at all times. If students roughhouse or get overly rambunctious, trying to push others off the mat, for example, eject them from the game for a few minutes (or longer, if the infractions are severe).

Teaching Tips

Take this game outside. Any soft surfaces, such as a beach or grassy field, will work well. (You may want to instruct students to wear old clothes if playing outside, particularly on grass.)

PASS PASS FOOTBALL

Number of Participants	Grade Level	Activity Level	Playing Area
2 teams of 5 to 8 players	6 and above	High	Football field

Recommended Equipment

- 1 football
- 1 jersey (or pinny) per player, one color for each team

Setup

This game is played on half a football field, using the 10-yard lines already marked. Divide students into teams and distribute the jerseys. Have each team select a quarterback (or students can take turns between plays).

Flip a coin to see who will kick off. The team that wins the coin toss (offense) begins on their 10-yard line.

How to Play

This game is like Touch Football (see page 170), except that 10-yard increments are used and multiple passes are allowed. (Other specific rules are listed below.) The team with the most points at the end of the game wins.

Rules

- The first pass must cross over the line of scrimmage.
- Once caught, the ball can be thrown again and again and again, until the ball carrier is tagged or throws an incomplete pass.

- On an incomplete pass, the ball is played from where the last pass was made.
- If the ball carrier runs across the first-down line (every 10 yards), play is stopped and the team gets a first down at that location. (The idea is to encourage players to throw.) If players throw the ball to a teammate past the 10-yard line, they can continue to advance the ball downfield.
- To count, touchdowns must be passed, not carried. If the ball is carried into the end zone, play is stopped, the ball is brought back to the 1-yard line, and the team gets 3 more downs to score a (passed) touchdown.

Safety Considerations

As in Touch Football, be sure to enforce the no-blocking rule.

Teaching Tips

To speed up the game and add some variety, use a Frisbee instead of a football. To make it easier for beginners to throw and catch the ball, try using a Throton, which is soft and shaped somewhat like a football. For more information about Throtons and where they can be purchased, contact Throtonics at (800) 343-0075.

INDOOR FOOTBALL

Number of Participants	Grade Level	Activity Level	Playing Area
2 teams of 3 to 5 players	8 and above	Medium	Basketball court

Recommended Equipment

- 1 football
- 1 set of flags per player
- 1 jersey (or pinny) per player, one color for each team

Setup

Designate the end zone: the 4 to 5 yards (meters) between the end of the court and the wall (or fence, if playing on an outdoor court).

Divide students into teams and distribute the jerseys. Have each team select a quarterback (or students can take turns between plays). Flip a coin to see which team will start. The starting team begins on their end zone line.

How to Play

Like Flag Football (see page 167), the objective in this game is to get more touchdowns than the other team. Unlike Flag Football, the offense gets 3 instead of 4 downs to score; quarterbacks have only 3 seconds (referee counts "1 steamboat, 2 steamboats, 3 steamboats") to initiate a play without obstruction from the defense; and no running plays are permitted. Other rules of flag football apply.

Safety Considerations

Be sure the end zone is far enough from walls so that students do not run into the wall when catching a pass. You may also want to add a rule about this: Players may not catch passes of more than 5 yards (meters) in the end zone.

Teaching Tips

For more fun, use scooters in the game. Students play while seated on scooters, which eliminates the risk of running injuries and falls but adds the potential for other accidents, including collisions, running over fingers and feet, and tipping over. Caution students to watch where they're going and to watch out for one another.

ULTIMATE FOOTBALL

Number of Participants	Grade Level	Activity Level	Playing Area
2 teams of 5 to 15 players	6 and above	High	Football field

Recommended Equipment

○ 1 football

○ 1 jersey (or pinny) per player, one color for each team

Setup

Divide students into teams and distribute the jerseys.

Flip a coin to determine which team will start and position the starting team behind their 30-yard line. The other team spreads out 20 to 40 yards (meters) further downfield.

How to Play

As in Touch Football (see page 170), the object is to score more points than the other team. In this game, however, there are no downs and players may pass the ball again and again. When a player with the ball is tagged or a pass is incomplete, the team must line up to kick the ball to the other team. Touchdowns (running into or catching a ball in the opponent's end zone) are worth 6 points, and field goals (throwing or kicking a ball into the opponent's end zone—without it being intercepted) are worth 2 points.

The starting team begins by kicking the ball downfield. The receiving team (offense) catches the ball and advances toward the other team's end zone.

Rules

1. For the opening kick, as well as kicks after a touchdown or field goal, all teammates must be behind the ball. If players are not behind the ball, a penalty is called and the other team gets the ball at the place of infraction.

2. If the kick is not caught, the receiving team scrambles to retrieve it and must then kick the ball back to the opposition, teammates lining up behind the ball (see Rule 1).

3. If an opponent intercepts the ball after it is kicked or thrown, that player may run the ball or pass it underhand (lateral pass) to a teammate. If the lateral pass is complete, the receiver can run the ball or pass it to a teammate, who can run the ball or pass it to a teammate, and so on. If the lateral pass is incomplete, the ball goes back to the passer, who must kick or throw it to the other team.

4. If a player is tagged (one hand) while carrying the ball, the ball is kicked to the other team. Before a ball is kicked to the opposing team, all teammates must be behind the kicker.

5. After a touchdown or field goal, the offense kicks the ball from their 30-yard (meter) line to the other team; teammates lined up behind the ball (see Rule 1 above).

If you have more students than the gym floor can accommodate, have students stand on the sidelines, where they can catch and deliver passes to teammates.

Safety Considerations

To avoid risk of injury, do not allow blocking, tackling, or rough play.

Teaching Tips

You can change this game significantly by using a Frisbee instead of a football and requiring players to throw the Frisbee rather than run with it.

Another variation to this game is Ultimate Scooter Football, which can be played indoors.

Ultimate Scooter Football

In this game, students play in a gym (or other indoor area) on scooters. To permit play within a confined area indoors, the following rules apply:

○ The ball must be passed into and caught in the end zone (demarcate a line at both ends of the gym).

- Players may not travel when in possession of the ball but must pass it within 3 seconds. In other words, the ball can only be advanced downfield by passing it to teammates.
- If the pass is incomplete, the other team gets the ball where it lands. If complete, the ball can be passed again and again.

1-DOWN FOOTBALL

Number of Participants	Grade Level	Activity Level	Playing Area
2 teams of 5 to 7 players	6 and above	Medium	Football field

Recommended Equipment

- 1 football
- 1 set of flags per player
- 1 jersey (or pinny) per player, one color for each team

Setup

This game is played on part of a football field, an area 30 yards (meters) long with an end zone at either end. Use flags, pylons, or other markers to designate the end zones.

Divide students into teams and distribute the jerseys. Flip a coin to see which team will start. One team gets the ball at centerfield (15 yards).

How to Play

This game is like Touch Football (see page 170), but each team gets only one opportunity (1 down) to score a touchdown. If they fail, the other team gets the ball at the spot where the player was tagged or, if the pass was incomplete, at the line of scrimmage. The team that gets the most touchdowns (worth 7 points) wins.

The rules of Touch Football apply, except

- at the kickoff and after a touchdown, the team starts the ball at centerfield and
- there are no field goals.

Safety Considerations

To prevent injury, do not allow blocking, tackling, or other rough play.

Teaching Tips

To make the game less challenging for younger or inexperienced students, use a Frisbee instead of a football.

chapter 11

Hockey Games

NON-CONTACT ICE HOCKEY

Number of Participants	Grade Level	Activity Level	Playing Area
2 teams of 6 to 15 players*	6 and above	High	Ice hockey rink

*if more than 6 players, make substitutions

Recommended Equipment

- 1 set of hockey pads (shin guards; and knee, elbow, and shoulder pads) per player
- 1 set of goalie pads (neck guard, and shin and body pads) per team
- 1 helmet (with face guard) per player
- 1 hockey stick per player
- 1 jersey (or pinny) per player, one color for each team
- 1 puck
- 1 whistle
- 1 pair hockey skates per player

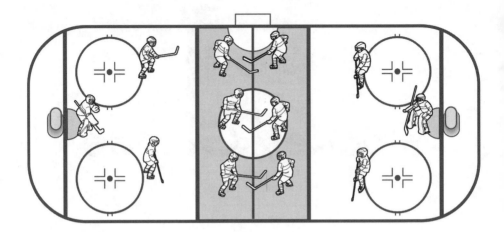

Setup

Divide students into teams and distribute the jerseys. Have the teams select 6 students (5 players and 1 goalie) to start on the ice and assign their positions (2 forwards, 1 center, 2 defense, and 1 goalie).

How to Play

This game is a simplified and gentler version of regular hockey: the rules aren't as technical and no checking or other contact between players is allowed. Games consist of two 20-minute halves or three 15-minute periods. Players try to score goals (each worth 1 point) by shooting the puck into the net of the opposing team. At the end of the game, the team with the most points wins.

At the start of the game, and after each goal, play starts with a face-off at center (the red line). In a face-off, the centers stand opposite each other and try to get control of the puck when the official drops it. (The puck must hit the ice before players can strike it.) After certain infractions (described next), the whistle is blown and face-offs are held in the offending team's defense zone (between the blue line and the goal line [where the net is set up]). In the case of rough play and more severe infractions (also described next), players must sit in the penalty box.

Rules

- *Icing* occurs when offensive players shoot the puck from their own defensive zone and it crosses the other team's goal line, and when the puck is 2 lines (red or blue) past the nearest player. In either case, a face-off is held in the offense's defensive zone.

- *Offsides* is called when a player enters the opposing team's defensive zone before the puck does. A face-off is held in that player's defensive zone.

- *Penalties* are called for high sticking (moving the hockey stick above the waist) and charging or deliberately touching other players (including touching them with hockey sticks). The offending player must sit in the penalty box for 3 minutes or until the opposition scores, whichever occurs first. For tripping, checking, elbowing, spitting, pulling a player's face mask, or other rough play, players must sit in the penalty box for 5 minutes, even if the opposition scores during that time.

If players get 3 3-minute penalties or 2 5-minute penalties during the game, this is considered misconduct and they must sit in the penalty box for 10 minutes or are ejected from the game.

- Goalies may use their hands and feet to stop the puck but must pass it with their sticks. If the goalie gloves a shot (holds the puck longer than 3 seconds), a face-off is held in that defensive zone.

- Goalies are the only players allowed in the goal crease. If an opposing player interferes with the puck in the crease, the other team gets a penalty shot.

- *Penalty shots.* The player who is fouled gets the puck at the blue line and can either shoot it from there or advance it down the ice to take a closer shot on the goalie. All other players must stay behind the blue line. If the penalty shooter misses the net, play continues. A goalie who catches or otherwise stops the puck rolls it to the side of the net, where a teammate takes it back into play.

- *Line changes.* If players get tired, they can switch positions with players on the bench at a stoppage in play. If substitutions are made during play the player going off the ice must come to the bench before the next player can go one the ice.

Safety Considerations

Make sure that all players wear full facemasks to protect their eyes. Because ice hockey is such a rapid game, it may be a good idea to have a qualified official referee.

Teaching Tips

If a player is hurt, stop play immediately and stop the clock. The clock should also be stopped for any breaks in the action during the last 2 minutes of the final period.

Increase the enjoyment and "level the playing field"—or the ice, in this case—by adding a few slight twists to the game.

Speed Hockey

This variation is the same as Non-Contact Hockey except that no line changes or player substitutions are allowed at the whistle.

No-Whistle Hockey

No whistles are used to stop play when the goalie freezes the puck. Instead, the goalie must always release the puck behind the net, where a teammate then has 5 seconds to skate or pass it out over the goal line. Opposing players must stay on the other side of the goal line during this time.

Sled Hockey

Instead of skates, use sleds designed for students with a disability. Players must sit on their sleds at all times during play.

INDOOR ICE HOCKEY

Number of Participants	Grade Level	Activity Level	Playing Area
2 teams of 6 to 15 players	6 and above	High	Gymnasium

Recommended Equipment

- ⊙ 1 set of goalie pads (neck guard, and shin and body pads) per team

- 1 helmet (with face guard) per player
- 1 hockey stick per player
- 1 jersey (or pinny) per player, one color for each team
- 2 carpet pieces per player
- 1 plastic puck or ball
- 1 whistle

Setup

Divide students into teams and distribute the jerseys. Have the teams select 6 students (5 players and 1 goalie) to start on the floor and assign their positions (2 forwards, 1 center, 2 defense, and 1 goalie).

How to Play

This game is like Non-Contact Hockey (see page 179) but with one major distinction. Because it is played indoors, players wear carpet squares (skates) on each foot to simulate the motion of skating on ice. Players must stay on their skates to play. If they touch the floor with their shoes, they cannot play the puck/ball till they get on their carpet pieces. At the end of the game, the team with the most points wins.

Safety Considerations

Helmets must be worn to protect players' eyes from sticks and the puck/ball.

Teaching Tips

Staying on the carpet squares is challenging. You can reduce player frustration by easing the rules a bit. For example, consider eliminating the offsides and icing rules to keep the game moving. You might also try Boot Hockey.

Boot Hockey

In this game, students wear their winter boots instead of carpet pieces and kick a tennis ball.

"POND" HOCKEY

Number of Participants	Grade Level	Activity Level	Playing Area
2 teams of 4 to 20 players	6 and above	High	Ice rink

Recommended Equipment

- 1 set of hockey pads (shin guards; and knee, elbow, and shoulder pads) per player
- 1 set of goalie pads (neck guard, and shin and body pads) per team
- 1 helmet (with face guard) per player
- 1 hockey stick per player
- 1 jersey (or pinny) per player, one color for each team
- 1 puck
- 1 whistle
- 1 pair hockey skates per player

Setup

Divide students into teams and distribute the jerseys. Have the teams assign positions (1 forward and 1 center [or 2 forwards], and 1 defense per line; 1 goalie per team).

How to Play

This game is similar to Non-Contact Hockey (see page 179), but with several modifications to encourage active play (see Rules). The game consists of two 15-minute halves. At the end of the game, the team with the most points wins.

Rules

- Each team has only 3 players to advance the puck, thus there is much more skating involved.
- Face-offs occur only at the start of each period, at the center of the rink.

- There are no box penalties in this game, but penalty shots are awarded for all infractions.
- Offsides and icing are not called.
- After a goal, the scoring team must retreat to their own side of the rink while the other team brings the puck out.

Safety Considerations

This game is rapid and students may become winded quickly. Allow frequent player substitutions. Rough play is usually not a factor here, simply because students are usually too tired or too far away from each other to engage in shenanigans.

Teaching Tips

Because there is so much skating involved, consider using a smaller ice rink for younger students. Outdoor rinks are usually smaller by 30 percent or more.

FLOOR HOCKEY

Number of Participants	Grade Level	Activity Level	Playing Area
2 teams of 6 or more players	4 and above	High	Gymnasium*

*or paved area (the size of a volleyball court or larger)

Recommended Equipment

- 1 floor hockey stick per player
- 1 pair of protective goggles per player (a helmet with a face mask would also work)
- 1 jersey (or pinny) per player, one color for each team
- 1 plastic puck
- 2 floor hockey nets
- 1 whistle

Setup

Place a net at both ends of the gym, 2 yards (meters) in front of the wall. Draw (or use tape to designate) a goal crease 1 yard (meter) in front of and to either side of the goal. Designate a "bench" (an area where teams sit when they are not playing) and a penalty box for each team.

Divide students into teams and distribute the jerseys. Have each team select 6 students (5 players and 1 goalie) to start on the floor and assign their positions (2 forwards, 1 center, 2 defense, and 1 goalie).

How to Play

This game is like Non-Contact Hockey (see page 179) but with several modifications to make it work off the ice. The object is to outscore the opposing team and no body contact is allowed. The rules of Non-Contact Hockey apply, with the following exceptions.

Rules

- Face-offs are used only to start play at the beginning of each period and after a goal is scored.
- For minor infractions (offsides, icing, and gloving the puck), the other team gets the puck and passes it in from the sideline.
- When the puck goes out of bounds, the last team to touch it loses control and the other team gets to pass it in from the sideline.

Safety Considerations

Use a "stop and pass" whistle to prevent students from running into walls. At the sound of the whistle, players must stop play and the player closest to the puck passes it in from the sideline.

To reduce the risk of shin injuries, have students wear shin (soccer) pads.

Teaching Tips

Be sure to call enough line changes that every student gets to play.

If you're short on floor hockey sticks, distribute sticks to the starters on each team. Then, during line changes, students drop their sticks where they are playing and substitutes pick them up. (This will help to ensure that only 5 players from each team are on the floor at one time.)

You can also use a tennis or whiffle ball in this game. To add more variety and challenge, or to intensify the action, try the following variations.

Quick-Sub Hockey

To accommodate more students, blow a whistle every 30 seconds during the game. At the sound of the whistle, the players on the floor go to the bench and the next line runs onto the floor. (This variation can be also applied to other games in this chapter.)

3-a-Side Hockey

Smaller gyms can get crowded with 11 players (everyone but the opposing team's goalie) on half the court. This game solves this problem. The forwards and center from each team play on the opposing team's side of the court (defensive zone). In other words, 6 players are on each side: 1 goalie, 2 defense, and 2 forwards and 1 center from the opposing team. If players are caught on the wrong side of the court, the offending players must sit out for 1 minute. This variation also helps to reduce rough play.

Foot Hockey

Instead of hitting a puck with floor hockey sticks, students kick a ball with their feet. Any size ball can be used, but given the instability of floor hockey nets, the lighter, the better.

SCOOTER NOODLE HOCKEY

Number of Participants	Grade Level	Activity Level	Playing Area
2 teams of 5 to 8 players	4 and above	Medium	Basketball court

Recommended Equipment

- 1 noodle (foam insulator) per player
- 1 jersey (or pinny) per player, one color for each team
- 1 scooter per player
- 3 whiffle balls
- 4 pylons

Setup

On each side of the court, place 2 pylons where the basketball key and the end line intersect—this is the goal. The sidelines of the court are the boundaries. Divide students into teams and have each team assign positions (2 to 4 defense, and 2 to 4 forwards). Distribute the jerseys, noodles, and scooters; then have students get on their scooters and into position.

How to Play

This game is like hockey, in that riding on scooters simulates the sensation of gliding across the ice, but it is far simpler to play. The obvious differences: players use (1) noodles instead of hockey sticks, (2) a whiffle ball instead of a puck, and (3) scooters instead of skates; and (4) there is no goalie.

Players hit the ball into the opposing team's goal, trying to outscore the opposing team. At the end of the game (two or three 15-minute periods, depending on class time), the team with the most points wins.

Rules

- At the start of each period and after each goal, instead of a face-off, the referee tosses the ball into the middle of the court (at the centerline) and players scoot to reach it.
- Players cannot advance the ball with their hands or feet, or when they are off their scooters. If they do, the referee picks up the ball and the other team takes it out from the sideline.
- If the ball goes out of bounds, the referee picks it up and throws it back into the playing area.
- Players are not allowed in the crease (the 3-point basketball arch). If the ball gets stuck in this area, the referee retrieves it and throws it back into play.
- No offsides, icing, or other infractions are called. When players engage in rough play (hitting others with noodles, deliberately colliding with opposing players, and so on), they must sit out of the game for 2 minutes or until the opposing team scores a goal, whichever occurs first.

Safety Considerations

Caution students to watch where they're going and to watch out for other students' fingers and toes.

Teaching Tips

It may be helpful to appoint a few referees (at least 1 on either side of the court) to keep the ball in play and watch for rough or unfair play.

You can also eliminate the noodles. Simply have players hit the ball with their hands. Using a large ball, such as a beach ball, may be a good idea for younger players.

BROOMBALL

Number of Participants	Grade Level	Activity Area	Playing
2 teams of 6 or more players	6 and above	High	Ice hockey rink

Recommended Equipment

- 1 broom per player
- 1 helmet (with face mask) per player
- 1 pair of broomball (or running) shoes per player
- 1 jersey (or pinny) per player, one color for each team
- 1 ball
- 2 sets of goalie pads (neck guard, and shin and body pads)

Setup

Divide students into teams and distribute the jerseys. Have the teams select 6 students to start on the ice and assign their positions (2 forwards, 1 center, 2 defense, and 1 goalie).

How to Play

Games consist of two 15-minute halves. Players try to score goals (each worth 1 point) by shooting the ball into the net of the opposing team. At the end of the game, the team with the most points wins.

Besides using brooms in place of hockey sticks and a ball in place of a puck, the rules are the same as in Non-Contact Hockey (see page 179), except there is no icing. When caught checking, high sticking, tripping, elbowing, and engaging in other rough play, players must sit out of the game for 2 minutes. Also, depending on the seriousness of the infraction, the other team gets a penalty shot or gets control of the ball at the place of infraction.

Safety Considerations

While safer than street shoes, broomball shoes can still be dangerous. Enforce the no-contact rules to prevent slips and falls.

Teaching Tips

If available, use broomball sticks. The bristles are either bound or made of plastic, which makes shooting a lot easier.

Increase the enjoyment and "level the playing field"—or the ice, in this case—by adding a few twists to the game.

Partner Broomball

In this variation, 2 students share a broom and both must have their hands on it to shoot the ball. This variation could also be applied to many of the hockey games in this chapter.

One-Pass Broomball

After passing the ball, students must sit down until 2 other teammates have touched the ball or the other team has taken possession. Be sure students watch out for the ball while they are seated.

Bladder Broomball

Use the bladder of a soccer ball. A ball bladder will not travel as quickly or as far, and its erratic movements make for an entertaining—not to mention challenging—game. In addition, there should be no goalie, and no player from either team is permitted into the goal crease.

chapter 12

Soccer Games

RECREATIONAL SOCCER

Number of Participants	Grade Level	Activity Level	Playing Area
2 teams of 11 or more players	4 and above	High	Soccer field

Recommended Equipment

- 1 jersey (or pinny) per player, one color for each team
- 1 black jersey (or pinny) per team
- 1 pair of shin guards per player
- 1 soccer ball

Setup

Divide students into teams and distribute the jerseys (each goalie gets a black jersey) and shin guards. Have each team select a goalie. Position teams on opposite sides of the field: 1 goalie in the goal, 3 defense in front of the goalie, 2 forwards and 1 center at centerfield, and 4 midfielders between the defense and forwards. (If you have more than 22 students in class, you'll have to work player substitutions into the game.) Flip a coin to see which team will start.

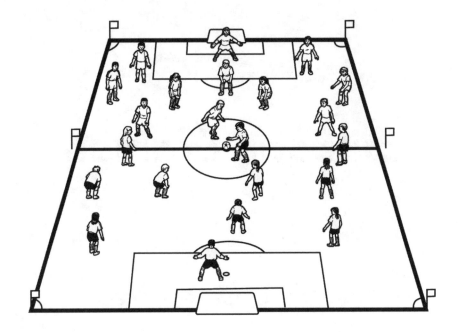

How to Play

Games consist of two 20-minute halves (or 30-minute halves, depending on class time). The team with the most points at the end of the game wins.

To begin, the referee places the ball in front of the center and then blows the whistle. At the sound of the whistle, the center passes it to a teammate. The first pass must be in the direction of the opponent's goal. Play continues until a team scores, at which point the other team gets the ball at center.

Rules

- Players must advance the ball with their feet, legs, torso, and head. Players are not allowed to use their hands or arms in any way. If the ball touches a player's hand or arm (from the fingertips to the shoulder), the opposing team gets a direct free kick.

- Goalies can touch the ball with their hands only when inside the penalty area (18 yards from the goal line). If they touch the ball with their hands outside this box or hold the ball longer than 3 seconds, the other team gets a direct free kick.

- Goalies may throw or kick the ball after they have caught it.
- If the ball deflects off the goalpost or the goalie, it is still in play.
- *Offsides* is called when forwards are between the ball and opposing team's goal. In other words, players may not stay at the opposing team's goal and wait for the ball to be passed to them. When offsides is called, the other team gets an indirect free kick.
- *Fouls* are called when players trip, bump, or check other players, or engage in other rough play. If the foul is deliberate, the fouled player gets a direct free kick. If unintentional (players sometimes run into and trip each other without meaning to), the fouled player gets an indirect free kick. If a foul occurs in the 18-yard (meter) box, the fouled player gets a penalty shot.
- *Free kicks.* There are two types of free kicks: direct and indirect. Both are taken at the point of the infraction. In a direct free kick, the ball may be kicked directly in the goal without it touching anyone else. The defense must stand 10 yards away from the ball. In an indirect free kick, the ball must contact another player before going into the goal. Defensive players must stand 10 yards away.
- *Penalty shots.* The ball is placed 12 yards (meters) in front of the goal and the kicker gets one kick. The goalie must stand on the goal line until the ball is kicked. All other players must stand outside the 18-yard (meter) box when the shot is taken. Once the ball is kicked, the ball is in play.
- When the ball goes out of bounds over a sideline, the team that kicked it out loses the ball and 1 player from the other team gets to throw it in from the sideline (at the spot it went out of bounds). When throwing the ball in, players must hold the ball with both hands behind their heads, then throw the ball directly to a teammate while keeping both feet on the ground.
- When the ball goes out of bounds over an end line, there are two options: (1) If the offense kicked it out over the defensive end line, the goalie places the ball on either corner

of the goal crease (whichever corner is closest to where the ball went out of bounds) and kicks it downfield. (2) If the defense knocked the ball out over their own end line, a corner kick is used to bring the ball back into play. A defensive player places the ball on the corner of the field (whichever corner is closest to where the ball went out of bounds) and kicks it to a teammate.

Safety Considerations

Be sure to inspect the entire playing field for any potentially hazardous debris, such as broken glass or stones, that might injure players.

Teaching Tips

To increase the amount of contact players get with the ball, use a smaller field and fewer players (7 per team). This is particularly helpful for keeping younger students interested in the game.

To add some variety and challenge to the game, try One-Touch Soccer.

One-Touch Soccer

In this game, players may only touch the ball once until it is touched by another player. That means, they may only kick the ball; they cannot dribble to advance it downfield. Other Recreational Soccer rules apply.

FRISBEE SOCCER

Number of Participants	Grade Level	Activity Level	Playing Area
2 teams of 10 or more players	4 and above	High	Soccer field

Recommended Equipment

- ⊙ 1 jersey (or pinny) per player, one color for each team
- ⊙ 1 Frisbee

Setup

Divide students into teams and distribute the jerseys. (If you have more than 20 students in class, you'll have to work player substitutions into the game.) Position teams on opposite sides of the field: 3 defense in front of the goalie, 2 forwards and 1 center at centerfield, and 4 midfielders between the defense and forwards. Flip a coin to see which team will start.

How to Play

This game is like Recreational Soccer (see page 193), except a Frisbee is used instead of a soccer ball and there is no goalie (unless you use a foam Frisbee). Students advance downfield by throwing the Frisbee. Thus, use of hands and arms is allowed. Otherwise, the rules and play procedure are the same as in Recreational Soccer, with the following exceptions:

- Students are not allowed in the goal crease. If the Frisbee lands in the crease without going into the goal, 1 player from the defense retrieves the Frisbee and passes it out of the area.
- When a pass is incomplete, the other team gets the Frisbee where it lands. (This helps prevent student pileups and rough play.)
- Players may not walk or run with the Frisbee; they must pass it to a teammate. If players hold onto the Frisbee longer than 3 seconds, the other team gets it at that spot on the field.

Safety Considerations

Be sure to inspect the entire playing field for any potentially hazardous debris, such as broken glass or stones, that might injure players. Use of safety glasses is also recommended.

Teaching Tips

To help students develop accuracy and increase the amount of contact they get with the Frisbee, play on a smaller field and reduce team size.

MASS OUTDOOR SOCCER

Number of Participants	Grade Level	Activity Level	Playing Area
2 teams or 30 to 75 players	4 and above	High	Soccer field or any large area*

*(there are no side lines)

Recommended Equipment

- 1 jersey (or pinny) per player, one color for each team
- 1 black jersey (or pinny) per goalie
- 10 soft balls (foam balls, ball bladders, or other)
- 10 pylons

Setup

Using 5 pylons per team, mark a goal line 30 to 50 yards (meters) long at either end of the field. Place the balls at centerfield.

Ask for 2 volunteers to count goals, then divide the remaining students into teams. Have players stand at their goal lines and have each volunteer stand to the side of either goal line.

How to Play

As in regular soccer, each team tries to outscore the opposing team by getting as many goals as they can. In this game, however, the potential for scoring goals is much, much higher. At the end of the game, the team with the most points wins.

Rules

- Players may not touch other players. Instead of free and penalty kicks, players caught touching other players must sit out for 1 minute. (Habitual offenders should be ejected from the game.)
- Players advance the ball using their legs, feet, torsos, and heads only—no hands or arms. If players touch the ball with

their hands or arms (even inadvertently), the other team gets that ball (at the point it was touched).

◎ Each team can have unlimited goalies.

◎ Goalies can use their hands, but only within 2 yards (meters) of the goal line. If they are farther from the goal line and touch a ball with their hands, the other team gets that ball.

◎ If the ball deflects off the goalpost or the goalie, it is still in play.

◎ A goal is scored when any ball crosses the goal line, but it must be at or below shoulder level. Each goal is worth 1 point. Goal counters keep track of each team's score.

◎ When a goal is scored, a goalie retrieves the ball and puts it back in play. (Other goalies will have to fill in while this goalie is retrieving the ball.)

Safety Considerations

Because there are so many balls in play at the same time, warn students to pay attention.

Teaching Tips

This game could also be played indoors. The end walls of the gym (or other confined area) are the goals, and balls can be played off the side walls.

For some added fun to the existing pandemonium, try Monster Ball Mass Soccer.

Monster Ball Mass Soccer

Add 1 or 2 large balls (1 yard [meter] in diameter or larger) to the mix. Players may touch these balls only with their arms and hands, and goals scored with these balls must be thrown between waist and shoulder level.

INDOOR SOCCER

Number of Participants	Grade Level	Activity Level	Playing Area
2 teams of 6 players	4 and above	High	Gymnasium

Recommended Equipment

- 1 indoor soccer or large soft ball
- 1 jersey (or pinny) per player, one color for each team
- 1 black jersey (or pinny) per team
- 2 indoor soccer goals

Setup

Place a goal at either end of the gym and tape a 9-yard (meter) penalty box in front of the goal (or use existing lines). Divide the gym in half and draw a centerline (or use an existing centerline).

Divide students into teams and distribute the jerseys. Flip a coin to determine which team will start. Have each team assign positions (1 goalie, 2 defense, and 3 forwards). If there are more than 12 students in class, have each team select 6 players to start and then work player substitutions into the game. Position each team on its own side of the playing area, forwards lined up and facing each other at center.

How to Play

This game is like Recreational Soccer (see page 193) but with a few modifications to accommodate indoor play. Namely, there are fewer players on the field at one time, and all walls are in play.

As in Recreational Soccer, each team tries to outscore the opposing team. The game consists of two 20-minute halves and begins with the team that won the coin toss taking the ball from the centerline. (The ball must travel over the centerline before it can be passed behind.) After a goal is scored, the other team gets the ball at center. Players advance the ball by kicking it "downfield," using only their legs, feet, torsos, and heads. At the end of the game, the team with the most points wins.

Rules

- The same player cannot kick the ball twice in a row. Someone else must contact the ball before a player can kick or touch it again.
- All walls, bleachers, and other side obstructions are in bounds—except the corners on either end of the gym. (Substitute players and teammates sit in one corner on each team's side and players who have to sit out of the game sit in the other corner on each team's side.)
- If the ball is knocked into a corner, the other team gets the ball. One player places it in the playing area and kicks it to a teammate. Note: Other players must give this player sufficient room.
- Substitutions can be made on the fly or after any goal.
- Players who deliberately bump, check, or trip other players, or engage in any kind of rough play, must sit out for 2 minutes.
- If the ball deflects off the goal or goalie, it is still in play—even if it hits the back wall.
- Goalies can touch the ball with their hands only when inside the penalty box. If they touch the ball with their hands outside this box or hold the ball longer than 3 seconds, the other team gets the ball at the centerline.
- Goalies must throw the ball—not kick it—once they have picked it up.

Safety Considerations

An indoor soccer ball can be hazardous for inexperienced goalies. Try using a foam ball or a ball bladder.

Teaching Tips

To reduce overcrowding on the floor, try Offensive Soccer. To add a new twist to the game, try Indoor Hand Soccer. To accommodate more students and add some real fun to the game, try Blind Soccer.

Offensive Soccer

In this game, students may not cross the centerline. Thus, only 6 players will be on each half at a time: 3 forwards (from the opposing team), 2 defense, and 1 goalie. This variation not only gives students more room to move, but it also reduces the risk of fighting for the ball and other roughhousing.

Indoor Hand Soccer

This is the same as Indoor Soccer, except students must advance the ball using only their hands. (If a leg, foot, or other part of the body inadvertently touches the ball, that's OK. If deliberate, the other team gets the ball at the point of infraction.) To prevent pushing and shoving, it is best not to allow dribbling or carrying. Students must catch the ball and immediately pass it to a teammate.

Blind Soccer

This game is played just like Indoor Soccer, except that students walk—not run—and half the students are blindfolded. Teammates work as partners: 1 blindfolded and the other without a blindfold. Blindfolded players are the only ones who can touch the ball. They advance it while their seeing counterparts direct them. (Seeing partners may also steer blindfolded players to prevent collisions.) Players walk the ball to reduce the risk of tripping, falling, and other injury. This variation can also be played outdoors.

NO-GOALIE INDOOR SOCCER

Number of Participants	Grade Level	Activity Level	Playing Area
2 teams of 5 or more players	4 and above	High	Basketball court

Recommended Equipment

- 1 indoor soccer ball
- 1 jersey (or pinny) per player, one color for each team
- 2 indoor soccer goals

Setup

Place a goal at either end of a gymnasium underneath a basketball hoop. The 3-point basketball arch is the goal crease. No one can enter this area. Divide students into teams and distribute the jerseys. Have teams select 5 players to start and assign positions (2 defense, 2 forwards, and 1 center). Flip a coin to determine which team will start with the ball.

How to Play

This game is like Indoor Soccer (see page 200), except there are no goalies. The starting team starts the ball at the centerline and tries to advance it toward the opposing team's goal using only their legs, feet, torsos, and heads. Players are not allowed to use their hands or arms (fingertips to shoulders) in any way. The team with the most points at the end of the game wins.

Indoor Soccer rules apply, except:

- No one is allowed in the goal crease, even to play the ball through it.
- If the ball lands and stays in the crease, the referee retrieves it and a defensive player kicks it downfield from the crease line.

- If an offensive player enters the crease, the defense gets a free kick. If a defensive player enters the crease, the offense gets a free kick.
- Free kicks are held at the centerline. Because there are no goalies in this game, a free kick consists of one kick only. No dribbling or otherwise advancing the ball is allowed. When a free kick is warranted, the referee places the ball on the centerline in front of the kicker. All other players must be behind the kicker, ready to rebound the ball should the kicker miss.
- After a goal, a player from the team scored upon starts the ball from the centerline.

Safety Considerations

Students may become frustrated or angry as the ball is traveling toward their unguarded net. Watch for aggression, and stop it before fights ensue.

Teaching Tips

If scores are too high, meaning the game is too easy, revise the crease rule somewhat. Allow the defense on each team to guard their goal, using their legs, feet, heads, and torsos only—they still cannot use their hands or arms.

To make the game more challenging, try Pin-Down Soccer.

Pin-Down Soccer

In this variation, a bowling pin is used as the goal instead of a net. Position the pin in the middle of the circle at the top of each basketball key. Players must knock it down to score. No students (offense or defense) are allowed in the circle.

FOUR-GOAL SOCCER

Number of Participants	Grade Level	Activity Level	Playing Area
4 teams of 5 to 7 players	4 and above	High	Gymnasium

Recommended Equipment

- 4 soft balls (foam or bladders)
- 1 jersey (or pinny) per player, one color for each team
- 8 pylons

Setup

Using 2 pylons, mark a goal in each corner of the gym. Each goal should be 2 yards (meters) wide. (Goal height is each goalie's shoulder level.)

Ask for 4 volunteers to count goals. Divide students into teams and distribute the jerseys. Have each team select a goalie. Position goalies and counters at each goal. The rest of the students scatter around the floor.

Note, if the gym is small or there are more than 28 students in class, you may have to work player substitutions into the game. Position the goals 3 yards (meters) from each corner and have substitute players stand behind the goals.

How to Play

The object of the game is to score as many goals as possible on any of the opposing team's goals. At the end of the game, the team with the fewest goals scored against them wins.

Play begins with the referee throwing all 4 balls into play. Players advance the ball using their feet, legs, torsos, and heads. No hand or arm contact is allowed, except for the goalies who may use their hands and arms within 2 yards (meters) of the goal.

Rules

As in Indoor Soccer (see page 200),

- All walls, bleachers, and other side obstructions are in bounds.
- Substitutions (if necessary) can be made on the fly.
- If the ball deflects off the goal or goalie, it is still in play. (But, if you are using the corner areas behind each goal for substitutes, these players can catch the ball and pass it to the goalie.)

- Goalies may use their hands and arms within 2 yards (meters) of the goal. If they touch the ball with their hands outside this area or hold the ball longer than 3 seconds after catching it, the other team gets the ball at center.
- Goalies must throw the ball—not kick it—once they have picked it up.

Safety Considerations

Foam or bladder balls will go a long way in preventing injuries, but this game moves quickly, and lots of balls are flying around. Caution students to watch out for one another.

Teaching Tips

Once they've played this game a few times, teams being scored against will start ganging up against the scoring team. Because it adds some strategy to the game and will likely result in a closer score, this should be encouraged. Have the counters call out each goal as it scored.

For younger children, who are often less accurate in their shots, it may be helpful to enlarge the goal size.

SCOOTER SOCCER

Number of Participants	Grade Level	Activity Level	Playing Area
2 teams of 6 to 8 players	4 and above	High	Gymnasium

Recommended Equipment

- 1 scooter per player
- 1 jersey (or pinny) per player, one color for each team
- 2 to 3 foam balls
- 2 indoor soccer goals

Setup

Place a goal at either end of the gym and tape a 9-yard (meter) penalty box in front of the goal (or use existing lines). Divide the gym in half and draw a centerline (or use an existing centerline).

Divide students into teams and distribute the jerseys and scooters. Have each team assign positions (1 goalie, 2 to 3 defense, and 3 to 4 forwards). If there are more than 16 students in class, have each team select 8 students to start and then work player substitutions into the game. Have students get into position, seated on their scooters, forwards lined up and facing each other at center.

How to Play

This game is similar to Indoor Soccer (see page 200) but with the following key differences: players (1) must be seated on their scooters at all times, and (2) may touch (but not propel) the balls with their hands and arms; and (3) more players, and balls, are on the floor at any given time.

The objective is to outscore the opposing team. Games consists of two 20-minute halves. To begin, players line up on their own side of the centerline and the referee tosses the balls into the middle of the "field." Players propel themselves with their legs, feet, and hands. They may advance the ball using their legs, feet, torsos, and heads—no hands or arms. After a goal is scored, the other team gets the ball at center. At the end of the game, the team with the most points wins.

Rules

- Players may not touch the balls with their hands and arms (fingertips to shoulders). If accidental, hand and arm contact is OK. If deliberate or used to advance the balls, however, the offending player has to sit out of the game for 1 minute and the other team gets that ball.

- All walls, bleachers, and other side obstructions are in bounds—except the corners on either end of the gym. (Substitute players and teammates sit in one corner on each team's side and players who have to sit out of the game sit in the other corner on each team's side.)

⊙ If a ball is knocked into a corner, the other team gets it at the sideline. The team player closest to that ball places it in the playing area and kicks it to a teammate. Note: Other players must give this player sufficient room.

⊙ Substitutions can be made on the fly or after any goal.

⊙ Players who deliberately bump into, collide with, or try to trip other players (including trying to knock them off their scooters), or engage in other rough play, must sit out for 2 minutes.

⊙ If the ball deflects off the goal or goalie, it is still in play—even if it hits the back wall.

⊙ Goalies may touch the ball with their hands only when inside the penalty box. If they touch the ball with their hands outside this box or hold the ball longer than 3 seconds, the other team gets the ball at the centerline.

⊙ Goalies must throw the ball—not kick it—once they have picked it up.

⊙ Goalies are the only players allowed inside the penalty box. If players accidentally glide into the box, they can continue play—as long as they scoot out immediately. If players deliberately enter the penalty box area, for example, to kick a goal or to wait for a pass, they must sit out for 2 minutes and the other team gets the ball at the centerline.

Safety Considerations

Because several balls are used in this game, play is rapid and can get confusing. With scooters added to the mix, the potential for injury is increased. Warn students to be careful and watch out for one another. Although students' hands should be nowhere near the floor, it is still a good idea to caution them to keep their fingers and toes out from under scooter wheels.

Teaching Tips

For younger students, or simply to add some variety and excitement to the game, use a giant ball (beach balls, or other inflatable balls, and large playground balls work well). In this game, students may advance the balls by kicking, pushing, and throwing.

SQUASHED SOCCER

Number of Participants	Grade Level	Activity Level	Playing Area
2 teams of 2 players	6 and above	High	Squash court

Recommended Equipment

- ⊙ 1 indoor soccer ball
- ⊙ 2 gymnastic mats

Setup

Fold the gymnastic mats and place them at either end of the court. These are the goals. Divide students into teams and flip a coin to determine which team will start.

How to Play

This game is an action-packed contest of 2-on-2 soccer. The object is to outscore the opposing team. Play begins with a free kick from the starting team's goal. At the end of the game, which consists of two 15-minute halves, the team with the most points wins. Note: Reserve several courts so that everyone can play.

Rules

- Players advance the ball using their feet, legs, torsos, and heads. No hand or arm contact is allowed.
- There are no goalies in this game, but either player can step into the goal area (gymnastic mat) to block the goal. When acting as goalies, players may contact the ball with their arms and hands.
- All walls are in bounds.
- If players deliberately bump, check, or trip other players, or engage in any kind of rough play, the other team gets a free kick (between the kicker and goalie—no other players are involved) from center court.

Safety Considerations

To reduce the risk of injury, particularly for inexperienced players, use soft balls instead of indoor soccer balls.

Teaching Tips

This game can be played in any confined area, for example, a racquetball court or a fenced-in tennis court (before the nets go up).

TEAM HANDBALL

Number of Participants	Grade Level	Activity Level	Playing Area
2 teams of 6 players	6 and above	High	Basketball court

Recommended Equipment

- 2 indoor soccer nets
- 1 foam ball (volleyball size)
- 1 jersey (or pinny) per player, one color for each team

Setup

Place a goal at the end of the basketball key on either end of the court. The 3-point arch is the goal crease.

Divide students into teams, distribute jerseys, and flip a coin to determine which team will start. Have each team assign positions (1 goalie, 2 defense, and 3 forwards). If there are more than 12 students in class, have each team select 6 students to start and work player substitutions into the game.

How to Play

The object of the game is to outscore the opposing team. Players advance the ball "downfield" by throwing it to teammates. Goals are scored by throwing the ball into the opposing team's goal. At the start of the game and after a goal is scored, play begins with a free throw from the centerline. At the end of the game, two 15-minute halves, the team with the most points wins.

Rules

- Players may not kick, bounce, or dribble the ball. Only passing and shooting are allowed.
- Players have 3 seconds to pass or shoot the ball, and may take no more than 3 steps when in possession of the ball.

Infractions result in the other team getting a free throw from the top of the opposing team's arch.

- To get control of the ball, players can intercept passes only. They are not allowed to knock the ball out of a player's hands.
- Goalies must throw the ball after they have caught it—they are not allowed to kick it.
- Goalies may not pass the ball past the centerline (lobbing the ball across the court). An infraction results in the other team getting a free throw from the top of the opponent's arch.
- Only the goalies are allowed inside the goal crease. If offensive players enter this area, the defense gets a free throw from the top of the arch on the offense's side. (Note: From a jump, offensive players may land in the crease, but they must throw the ball before they land.) If defensive players enter this area, the offense gets a free throw from the top of the defense's arch.
- Tripping and holding result in a 2-minute penalty, as does having too many players on the court (if using player substitution). Body checking and other rough play results in a 5-minute penalty.
- *Free throws.* Free throws are between the thrower and the goalie. No other player may help block the goal. Free throws are held from the centerline or the top of the 3-point arch.
- *Penalties.* The offending player must sit out of the game (the other team has the advantage).
- If the ball is dropped or touches the ground (for example, after an incomplete pass or a failed interception), the last team to touch it loses the ball and the opposing team takes it in from the sideline.
- When the ball goes out of bounds over a sideline, the team that threw it out loses the ball and 1 player from the opposing team gets to throw it in from the sideline (at the spot it went out of bounds). When throwing the ball in, players must hold the ball with both hands behind their heads, then throw

the ball directly to a teammate while keeping both feet on the ground.

⊙ When the ball goes out of bounds over an end line, there are two options: (1) If the offense threw it out over the defensive end line, the goalie takes it to either corner of the crease (whichever corner is closest to where the ball went out of bounds) and throws it downfield to a teammate. (2) If the defense threw the ball out over their own end line, a defensive player throws the ball in from the corner of the field (whichever corner is closest to where the ball went out of bounds).

Safety Considerations

To minimize body contact, which inevitably leads to roughhousing and even injury, enforce the "interception only" rule by imposing a 10-minute penalty on students who habitually interfere with other players.

Teaching Tips

To increase the fun, use a foam Frisbee instead of a foam ball. For a real challenge, try Pinned-Down Team Handball.

Pinned-Down Team Handball

In this game, there are no goals or goalies. Instead, bowling pins are placed where the goals would normally be. The object is to knock down the opposing team's pin. This can be quite challenging with a foam ball. If younger players have difficulty hitting 1 pin, place 2 or 3 pins in the goal crease to increase the size of the target, but be sure to place them far enough apart that the other pins do not support the one being hit.

chapter 13

Volleyball Games

RECREATIONAL VOLLEYBALL

Number of Participants	Grade Level	Activity Level	Playing Area
2 teams of 6 players	6 and above	Medium	Volleyball court

Recommended Equipment

- 1 volleyball

Setup

Set the net height. For men, standard height is approximately 2.50 yards (meters); for women, approximately 2.25 yards (meters).

Divide students into teams. (If there are more than 12 students in class, set up more than 1 court and substitute a new player in at each rotation.) Have the teams get into position (2 lines of 3 students) on either side of the net and flip a coin to see which team will start.

How to Play

There is no time limit to the game. The first team to get 25 points wins. A team must win by 2 points. Matches are generally

2 out of 3, but if games are played quickly, students could play 3 out of 5 or 5 out of 7. In the last game of a match, teams switch sides when the first team reaches 8 points, and the first team to get 15 points (winning by 2) wins the game.

The starting team serves the ball over the net and into play. The opposing team gets three chances to hit the ball back over the net. The volley continues until a team is unable to return the ball. If the serving team loses the volley (is unable to return the ball), the other team gets the serve. If the other team loses the volley, the serving team gets 1 point and the same player serves again. The first team to get 25 (or 15 in the last game of a match) points wins.

Rules

Serving

- The player in the back right corner serves the ball for each team.
- When a team gets the serve, players rotate 1 position clockwise.
- Servers must serve from behind the back court line. Underhand and overhand serves are allowed.
- If not hit by a player on the opposing team, the ball must land in the opposing court. If the ball lands on the line, it is considered in.

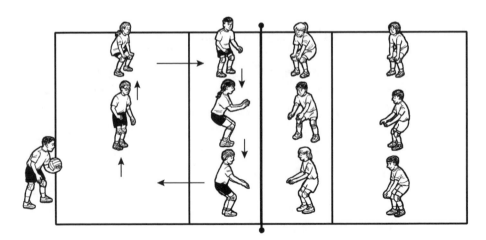

◎ If the ball hits the net, the server gets one chance to serve it again. After the second unsuccessful attempt, the other team gets the serve.

Volleying

◎ Only the serving team can score points. If the opposing team wins the volley, they get the serve.

◎ Teams get up to three hits (contacts with the ball) to return the ball over the net.

◎ The same player cannot hit the ball twice in a row. Another player must contact the ball.

◎ Players must strike the ball, not push or throw it.

◎ Players may not touch the net. If they do, the other team gets the point or the serve, depending on which team is serving.

◎ A back-row player may not contact the ball above the height of the net in front of the attack line (either to hit or block).

Safety Considerations

Be sure to pad the volleyball posts so that students will not hurt themselves if they run into a post.

Teaching Tips

For shorter games, limit the time to 25 minutes (or some other timeframe). In a timed game, the team with the highest score at the end of the game wins.

To include more students in the game, try Add-3 Volleyball and Pairs Volleyball. For inexperienced students, Underhand Volleyball is a good introduction to the game. For more experienced players, try Solo Volleyball. And to "level the playing field," try Capped-Serves Volleyball and Co-Ed Volleyball.

Add-3 Volleyball

This variation accommodates teams of 9 players (3 rows of 3) and is best suited to young and inexperienced students, who may have more trouble covering the court. The same rules apply, but rotation differs. Instead of a straight clockwise rotation, students rotate in a backward S pattern. Starting with the server, the back row moves to the left, then forward to the middle row, then to the right, then up to the front row, then to the left. The last player in the front row (on the left) moves diagonally back to the server position.

Solo Volleyball

Divide the court into narrow thirds (each small court straddles the net). Individuals compete against individuals. Regular volleyball rules apply, except individual players may contact the ball 3 consecutive times on their own side. This variation is best suited to skilled players.

Underhand Volleyball

The is the same as Recreational Volleyball except that all hits (serves and passes) must be underhand. Underhand serves are not only more likely to make it over the net but also easier to return and, therefore, less intimidating for inexperienced and young students.

Capped-Serves Volleyball

In this variation, each server is allowed a maximum of 5 consecutive serves, then the team must rotate and another teammate serves. If you have several strong servers in class, limit the number of consecutive serves further, say 3 or 4. Note: You could also limit a team to 5 consecutive points. Once a team scores 5 points, the other team gets the serve.

Co-Ed Volleyball

This variation requires that each team be balanced by gender: 3 males and 3 females on a 6-player team. (If playing Add-3 Volleyball, teams must comprise 4 females and 4 males, plus another player of either gender.) In addition, set the net height to the standard for women (see Setup), and add a rule that males may only spike (hit the ball over their head) from behind the attack line.

PASS VOLLEYBALL

Number of Participants	Grade Level	Activity Level	Playing Area
2 teams of 6 to 8 players	4 and above	Medium	Volleyball court

Recommended Equipment

- 2 or 3 volleyballs

Setup

Divide students into teams and have them take their positions on either side of the net. Flip a coin to see which team will start.

How to Play

This game is just like Recreational Volleyball (see page 215) but with a few modifications:

- Several balls are in play at one time.
- There can be 4 players in each row rather than 3.
- Players must catch and pass the ball—not hit it.
- If the ball is not caught, the other team gets the point or serve.
- Each team gets two chances to return the ball to the opposing team. If, for example, back-row players catch the ball, they can pass it to a front-row player who returns it to the opposing team's side of the net.
- Players must pass the ball underhand.

Safety Considerations

Be sure to pad the volleyball posts so that students don't hurt themselves if they run into a post.

Teaching Tips

For extra fun and competition, have 1 player from each team stand on the opposing team's side of the court. If these players catch the ball, their team gets the point (or serve).

FOLLY BALL

Number of Participants	Grade Level	Activity Level	Playing Area
2 teams of 6 players	6 and above	Medium	Volleyball court

Recommended Equipment

- 1 volleyball

Setup

Divide students into teams and have them take their positions on either side of the net. Flip a coin to see which team will start.

How to Play

This game is just like Recreational Volleyball (see page 215) but with a slight twist to the rotation. Instead of a clockwise rotation on each side of the court, players rotate to the opposing team in an M pattern (see illustration).

Starting at the back right corner of the court (the serving position), a player would rotate to the left twice, then forward once, then to the right twice. Rather than go back to the serving position, however, the player would move forward, under the net to the opposing team's side. From there, the player would rotate to face the net, then continue rotating to the right twice, then backward once (to the opposing team's serving position), then to the left twice. At that point, the player goes back to the original (serving) position.

All other Recreational Volleyball rules apply. The first team to get 25 points wins.

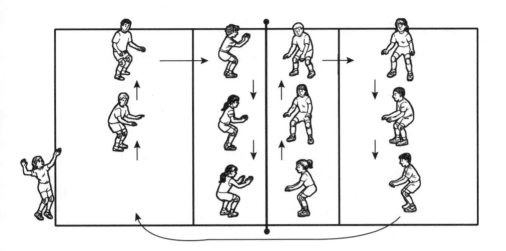

Safety Considerations

While not an issue of physical safety, players may be antagonistic toward one another, particularly if a student who just lost the volley is rotating to the opposing team. Do not allow students to rebuke or antagonize each other.

Teaching Tips

To lessen the competitiveness in the game even more, add a simple modification. The ball is served only from one side. When the serving team fails to get a point, everyone rotates and a new server takes over.

BLIND VOLLEYBALL

Number of Participants	Grade Level	Activity Level	Playing Area
2 teams of 6 players	6 and above	Medium	Volleyball court

Recommended Equipment

- 1 volleyball
- 1 tarp

Setup

Hang a tarp over the net and divide students into teams. Have them take their positions on either side of the net and flip a coin to see which team will start.

How to Play

This game is just like Recreational Volleyball (see page 215) but slightly more challenging. Because the tarp obstructs their view, players cannot see what is happening on the other side of the net. Recreational Volleyball rules apply, except that overhand serves and spikes are not permitted. The first team that gets 25 points wins.

Safety Considerations

Do not allow students to touch the tarp or poke it into students playing on the other side of the net.

Teaching Tips

In this game, rallies typically last longer if the ball is kept low so that the opposing team cannot see it. You can let students in on this strategy or let them figure it out for themselves.

ENORMOUS VOLLEYBALL

Number of Participants	Grade Level	Activity Level	Playing Area
2 teams of 8 to 16 players	8 and above	High	Volleyball court

Recommended Equipment

⊙ 1 large ball (1 or more yards [meters] in diameter)

Setup

Divide students into teams and have them take their positions on either side of the court. Flip a coin to determine which team will serve first.

How to Play

As in Recreational Volleyball (see page 215), each team tries to outscore the opposing team. The only differences are the following:

- ◎ A larger ball is used. Larger balls, while easier to hit, are more difficult to aim and propel over the net.
- ◎ Games go to 11 points. The first team to get 11 points (winning by 2 points) wins.
- ◎ A team gets up to five chances to return the ball to the opposing team's side.

Safety Considerations

Elbow and wrist strains can result if students hit the ball incorrectly. Demonstrate proper hitting technique (closed fist, hands together) before the game.

Teaching Tips

Depending on the age and height of your students, you may want to disallow overhand serves and spikes.

For some real fun, try Double Enormous Volleyball.

Double Enormous Volleyball

In this game, 2 large balls are in play at the same time. Each team serves a ball at the same time. If they collide, the serve is done over. Students volley as they normally would, but they must watch out for 2 balls instead of 1. When a point is scored, the other ball is out of play and teams serve again. This game can get confusing, particularly when both balls end up on 1 team's side, but is sure to be a crowd pleaser.

TOWEL VOLLEYBALL

Number of Participants	Grade Level	Activity Level	Playing Area
2 teams of 12 players	4 and above	Medium	Volleyball court

Recommended Equipment

○ 1 volleyball
○ 1 towel per 2 players

Setup

Divide students into teams and have each team get into position.

How to Play

This game is just like Recreational Volleyball (see page 215), except players are paired up, each pair holding a towel, and must volley the ball using the towel. Recreational Volleyball rules apply, with the following modifications:

○ Pairs serve the ball from the back court line using the towel.
○ To volley, players must catch and throw the ball with the towel.
○ The ball cannot be held or carried in the towel. Pairs must receive the ball (in a down motion) and release it back into play (in an up motion) within 3 seconds.
○ Each team gets three chances to return the ball.
○ If the ball rolls off the towel, or goes out of bounds, the opposing team gets the point or serve.

Safety Considerations

Do not allow students to snap the towels at each other.

Teaching Tips

For a little variety and to make the game easier for younger or less-skilled students, use a rubber chicken instead of a volleyball. To make the game more challenging, use 2 balls instead of 1.

FOUR-COURT VOLLEYBALL

Number of Participants	Grade Level	Activity Level	Playing Area
4 teams of 6 players	6 and above	Medium	Volleyball court

Recommended Equipment

- 1 volleyball
- 3 volleyball nets (with 5 posts to hold them up)

Setup

Divide the volleyball court into quadrants: in addition to the regular net that divides the court in half, put up 2 other nets to divide each half in half again. (The nets should form a cross.)

Divide students into teams and assign each team one of the 4 quadrants. Flip a coin to determine which team will serve first.

How to Play

This game is like Recreational Volleyball (see page 215), except 4 teams are playing at once and the object of the game is to get

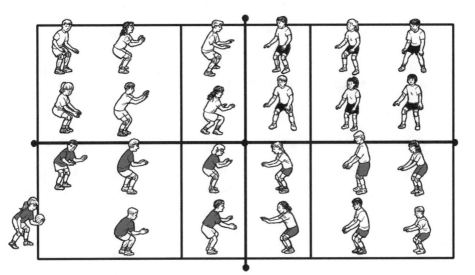

the lowest score. Games last 20 minutes. At the end of the game, the team with the fewest points wins.

Recreational Volleyball rules apply, with the following modifications:

- ☉ The team that loses the volley—not the serving team—gets 1 point.
- ☉ The team that wins the volley (the team that volleyed it into the last team's quadrant) gets the next serve.
- ☉ Once a team has been scored on, the serving team must serve the ball into one of the other quadrants.

Safety Considerations

Make sure all posts are properly padded.

Teaching Tips

To make the game easier for younger or less-skilled players, use a beach ball or other inflatable object. A beach ball is very light and will stay afloat longer.

SOCCER VOLLEYBALL

Number of Participants	Grade Level	Activity Level	Playing Area
2 teams of 2 to 4 players	10 and above	High	Volleyball court

Recommended Equipment

- ☉ 1 soccer ball

Setup

Adjust the net to 1 yard (meter) high. Divide students into teams and position them on either side of the net. Flip a coin to see which team will serve first.

How to Play

This game is like Recreational Volleyball (see page 215), but players use their feet, legs, torsos, and heads—not their arms or hands—to volley and return the ball.

In addition, the ball can bounce once between kicks. An example of a progression: the ball comes over the net, the receiving player kicks it, the ball bounces, then a teammate knees it up in the air, and another teammate kicks it up and over the net.

Like Recreational Volleyball, play begins with a serve from behind the back court line. In this game, however, the serve is a kick. Each side gets three chances to return the ball. If the ball touches a player's hands or arms, the opposing team gets the point or serve. The first team to get 25 points wins.

Safety Considerations

This game includes fewer players per team to allow students sufficient kicking room. To accommodate more players, use alternates and substitute players or set up several courts. To reduce the number of falls, caution players not to kick too high.

Teaching Tips

This game requires fairly well-developed soccer skills. To make it more challenging, should you have experienced soccer players in class, eliminate the bounces between kicks.

NOODLE VOLLEYBALL

Number of Participants	Grade Level	Activity Level	Playing Area
2 teams of 6 to 9 players	4 and above	High	Volleyball court

Recommended Equipment

- 1 foam noodle per player
- balloons

Setup

Divide students into teams and position them on either side of the net. Distribute the noodles to each player and give 2 balloons to each team.

How to Play

This game is a lot like Recreational Volleyball (see page 215), except (1) players volley balloons instead of volleyballs, (2) players hit the balloons with noodles rather than their hands, (3) there are more balloons in play at one time, and (4) the first team to get 15 points wins.

At the signal to start, teams hit their balloons over the net. Each team has three chances to bat each balloon back over the net. As in Recreational Volleyball,

- players may not bat the balloon twice in a row.
- if the balloon touches the ground or goes out of bounds, the other team gets 1 point.

Other Recreational Volleyball rules apply, with the following modifications:

- Only noodles may contact the balloons. Players may not touch the balloons with any part of their body. If they do, the other team gets 1 point.
- There is no formal service in this game. After a point is scored, the player nearest that balloon picks it up and bats it over the net to resume play.

Safety Considerations

Do not allow students to hit one another with the noodles. Although they are soft and will not cause injuries, caution should still be used. Likewise, do not let students get overly rambunctious with the balloons (i.e., popping them near other students' ears, stepping on them to pop them, and so on). To eliminate the temptation in younger and rowdy students, consider adding another rule to the game: The first team to pop a balloon loses the game.

Teaching Tips

Make this game easier by lowering the net and reducing the size of the playing area. To speed up the game, increase the number of balloons. Teams will reach 15 in no time!

chapter 14

Water Games

INNER TUBE WATER POLO

Number of Participants	Grade Level	Activity Level	Playing Area
2 teams of 3 to 6 players	6 and above	High	Swimming pool

Recommended Equipment

- 1 inner tube per participant
- 1 bathing cap per player, one color for each team
- 1 water polo ball
- 2 water polo nets

Setup

Place a water polo goal on either end of the pool. Divide students into teams and distribute the inner tubes and caps. Have students mount their tubes on the edge of the pool.

How to Play

The object of the game is to outscore the opposing team. The game begins with team members lined up on the edge of their own end of the pool. The referee throws the ball into the middle of the pool and players paddle to get to the ball. Players advance the ball using only their hands. Players may pass the ball or paddle it down the pool themselves, but they must pass it before shooting a goal (see Rules).

Rules

- Players must hit the ball with open hands, like paddles, not closed fists. If a player punches the ball, the other team gets a penalty shot.
- No positions are played in this game, but players should not congregate at one end of the pool. If more than 2 players (4 players if using 6-player teams) are on the opponent's half of the pool, the other team gets the ball from the center.
- For goals to count, the ball must be completely inside the goal and shooters must be on their tubes.
- Shooters must be past the center of the pool to shoot for a goal, and at least 2 offensive players must have contacted the ball before it was shot.
- No "running" or rough play is allowed. If players push off from the bottom of the pool (to propel themselves faster through the water), or hold or overturn an opponent's tube, the other team gets a penalty shot.
- Penalty shots allow a player to get the ball and either take a shot or pass the ball. Defensive players must be 5 yards (meters) from the thrower.
- Games consist of two 7- to 12-minute halves with a halftime break of 1 to 5 minutes. At the end of the game, the team with the most points wins.

Safety Considerations

If playing with real inner tubes, be sure to tape the stems to avoid skin irritations and scratches.

Teaching Tips

To accommodate more students at one time, increase team size and use 2 or 3 balls at the same time.

TOUCH INNER TUBE BALL

Number of Participants	Grade Level	Activity Level	Playing Area
2 teams of 5 to 7 players	8 and above	High	Swimming pool

Recommended Equipment

- 1 football
- 1 bathing cap per player, one color for each team
- 1 inner tube per player
- 4 buoys

Setup

Use 2 buoys to mark an end zone at each end of the pool. Divide students into teams and distribute the bathing caps and inner tubes. Have players mount their tubes on the edge of the pool and get into position. Flip a coin to see which team will start. The starting team begins 2 yards in front of their end zone.

How to Play

This game is like Touch Football (see page 170), except it is played on inner tubes in a pool, multiple passes are allowed, and yard counts are not used. Instead, each team gets 6 downs to reach the opponent's end zone. Other specific rules are listed here.

The game consists of two 15- to 20-minute halves. At the last minute of each half, call out "One minute remaining!" Then stop the clock between plays for the rest of the half. Allow a 2-minute break at halftime. The team with the most points at the end of the game wins.

Rules

- Players propel themselves with their feet and hands, paddling and kicking down the pool.

- Players carrying the ball may either pass it, "run" with it by carrying the ball in their laps, or a combination of both.
- Once caught, the ball can be passed again and again and again, until the ball carrier is tagged or throws an incomplete pass.
- On an incomplete pass, the ball is played from where the last pass was made.
- Touchdowns must be passed, not carried. If the ball is carried into the end zone, play is stopped, the ball is brought back to 1 yard from the end zone, and the team gets its remaining downs to score a (passed) touchdown.
- To stop a ball carrier, defensive players must tag them by holding onto their tubes.
- Rough play, including tipping or colliding into other players' tubes, is not allowed. The offending player's team gets a half-pool penalty. In other words, the offense advances halfway down the pool to start the next play.

Safety Considerations

One of the main purposes of the buoy line is to prevent players from banging into the edge of the pool. Caution players to coast once in the end zone.

Teaching Tips

Instead of using a football, try a beach ball or other inflatable object.

INNER TUBE BASKETBALL

Number of Participants	Grade Level	Activity Level	Playing Area
2 teams of 5 players	8 and above	High	Swimming pool

Recommended Equipment

- 1 inner tube per player
- 1 bathing cap per player, one color for each team
- 2 pool basketball hoops
- 1 buoyant ball

Setup

Set up a basketball hoop at either end of a pool. Divide students into teams and distribute the inner tubes and caps. Have students mount their tubes on the edge of the pool by their team's basket.

How to Play

This game is like Scooter Basketball (see page 162), except it is played on inner tubes in a pool instead of on scooters. Teams try to outscore each other (each field shot is worth 2 points; foul shots are worth 1 point). At the end of the game, the team with the most points wins.

The game begins with the referee throwing the ball into the middle of the pool. Both teams paddle to retrieve the ball. From there, Scooter Basketball rules apply, with the following modifications:

- If players run into each other or impede other players' tubes in any way, fouls are called (offensive, defensive, or technical, depending on who initiated the foul).
- Players have 3 seconds to pass or shoot the ball. If a player holds onto the ball, the other team gets it where the infraction occurred.
- After a basket is scored, the team scored upon has 10 seconds to get the ball underway.

Safety Considerations

To prevent accidental tips and collisions, do not allow players to congregate in any area of the pool.

Teaching Tips

This game could be played without inner tubes in a shallow pool (1 yard [meter] deep or less).

POOL PUSH

Number of Participants	Grade Level	Activity Level	Playing Area
2 players per team	6 and above	Low	Swimming pool

Recommended Equipment

- 1 rubber dinghy per team

Setup

Divide students into teams and line them up along one side of the pool. Have 1 team member sit on a dinghy in the water at the pool's edge and the other on the pool deck.

How to Play

At the signal to start, the players on deck push their partner's dingy. The dinghy that drifts the farthest wins.

Safety Considerations

Lifeguards should be ready and on the lookout for students who tip over in their dinghies.

Teaching Tips

If the pool is too small for everyone to participate at once, use distance markers to keep track of the farthest drifts.

It's a good idea to ask students whether they are comfortable in the water. Those who are not should stay on the pool deck and be the pushers.

POOL PADDLE

Number of Participants	Grade Level	Activity Level	Playing Area
Any number	8 and above	High	Swimming pool

Recommended Equipment

- 1 rubber dinghy per player
- 1 paddle per player

Setup

Distribute dinghies and paddles to students. Have students get in their dinghies along the edge of the pool and hold onto the pool edge.

How to Play

At the signal to start, players release the pool edge and paddle their dinghies to the other side of the pool. The first one to touch the opposite pool edge is the winner.

Safety Considerations

To prevent accidental tips, do not allow students to push off from the pool edge.

Teaching Tips

If you do not have enough dinghies (or space in the pool) for everyone to participate, time each student separately. The student with the fastest time wins.

To add a little variety to the race, line up half the students on one side of the pool and the other half on the other side. At the signal, students must paddle across the pool. The one who crosses first (likely the one who manages to avoid the other dinghies) wins.

chapter 15

Winterfest

• • • • • • • •

FROZEN SNOWBALLS

Number of Participants	Grade Level	Activity Level	Playing Area
2 teams of 10 or more players	4 and above	Medium	Basketball court

Recommended Equipment

- 1 large cardboard "freezer" box per team
- 1 sock per participant

Setup

Divide students into teams and position them on opposite halves of the playing area. Give each student a "snowball" (folded-up sock). Open a cardboard freezer box and flip it upside-down in the middle of each basketball key.

How to Play

The game lasts 1 to 2 minutes. At the signal to start, players shoot their snowballs at the opposing team's freezer.

Players may not cross the centerline or enter the key at any time. If they do, the other team gets to take 1 snowball out of their freezer. At the end of the game, the team with the fewest snowballs in their freezer wins.

Safety Considerations

Watch that students do not throw socks at each other. If students are caught throwing snowballs directly at other students, their teams must put 1 snowball into their own freezers (use a snowball that missed the box).

Teaching Tips

For more action, divide the gym into quadrants and students into 4 teams. Mark a key (use tape or pylons) and place a freezer box in each quadrant. At the signal to start, students throw snowballs into any of the other teams' freezers. Students are not allowed to leave their own quadrant. At the end of the game, the team with the fewest snowballs in their freezer wins.

This game can also be played outdoors, using real snowballs and snow forts as the freezers. Give teams 10 minutes to design their forts (ideally to restrict snowball entry) and then play the game for 20 or 30 minutes, depending on class time.

SNOW SCULPTURE CONTEST

Number of Participants	Grade Level	Activity Level	Playing Area
2 or more teams of 3 to 5 players	4 and above	Low	Snowy area

Recommended Equipment

○ 1 shovel (or trowel) per team

Setup

Ask for 3 to 5 volunteers to judge the snow sculptures. Divide students into teams and distribute a copy of the rules to each team.

Designate an area, 10 square yards (meters), in which teams build their sculptures.

How to Play

This contest can be run over several days (72 hours is recommended), several hours, or within a single class period. Within the predesignated timeframe, teams compete to produce the most impressive snow sculpture.

Rules

Sculpting

- Bracing and other structural supports are not permitted.
- Sculptors must start at the same time. No starting early.
- Coloring and use of props (i.e., clothing, hats, flags, etc.) are not permitted.
- Only 1 trowel may be used per team.
- Sculptors must stay in their defined area.

Judging

Up to 5 points are awarded for each of the following criteria:
- Degree of difficulty
- Originality
- Detail
- Impact (the "wow" factor)
- Size

Safety Considerations

To reduce the risk of falls, do not allow students to use ladders to work on their sculptures.

Teaching Tips

If there is a chance that structures will melt or be vandalized if left overnight, limit the contest to a few hours or within a single class period.

During summer months, or for those in warm climates, hold a sand-sculpting contest.

Developing a contest theme can add some excitement to the activity. For example, if this contest will be one of many Winterfest activities planned for the winter months, require students to build a sculpture that reflects the winter theme. (Then add "Interpretation of theme" to the judging criteria.)

SNOW BOWL

Number of Participants	Grade Level	Activity Level	Playing Area
Any number	4 and above	Low	Snowy area

Recommended Equipment

⊙ 6 bowling pins

Setup

Place the bowling pins upright in a triangle formation (rows of 1, 2, and 3 pins), approximately 4 inches (10 centimeters) apart. Mark a starting line on the snow 5 yards (meters) away. Line up students in single file behind this line and have them make their snowballs.

How to Play

The object of this game is to knock down all 6 bowling pins. One at a time, players throw their snowballs at the pins. The player who knocks them down in the fewest throws wins.

Safety Considerations

Do not allow students to stand behind the pins or throw snowballs at each other while waiting in line.

Teaching Tips

To speed up the game, have students throw 3 snowballs each. The student who knocks the most pins down in 3 throws (or knocks all the pins down in the fewest throws) wins. In the event of a tie, have a "bowl off."

CURLING FUNSPIEL

Number of Participants	Grade Level	Activity Level	Playing Area
2 teams of 4 players	8 and above	Low	Curling rink

Recommended Equipment

- 16 curling stones (2 color per team)
- 1 curling broom per player

Setup

Divide students into teams and have them number off (1, 2, 3, and 4 on each team). Distribute the curling stones, 2 stones of the same color to each student on a team, and flip a coin to determine which team will throw first.

How to Play

This game is like regular curling but with a few modifications to the delivery rules. Players either *throw* the stones with their hands or *deliver* them by pushing them with the curling brooms. The target: the circles at the end of the rink.

Alternating between teams and following their team number (1, 2, 3, or 4), players throw or deliver 2 stones in each *end* (like an inning in baseball). For example: Player 1 from Team A (Player A1) throws/delivers his first stone; Player 1 from Team B (Player B1) throws/delivers her first stone; Player A1 throws/delivers his second stone; and Player B1 throws/delivers her second stone. Then Player 2 from Team A (Player A2) throws/delivers her third stone; Player 2 from Team B (Player B2) throws/delivers his third stone; and so on.

This sequence—totaling 16 throws/deliveries or 8 throws/deliveries per team (2 stones per player)—constitutes 1 end. A match consists of 4 ends.

Delivery and Throwing

Typically a player delivers a stone with one hand. If the stone needs to go further, 2 players on the throwing team may sweep the ice in front of the stone.

End 1

- ◉ Stone 1: Regular delivery, but no sweeping is permitted
- ◉ Stone 2: Throw with right hand

End 2

- ◉ Stone 3: Throw with left hand
- ◉ Stone 4: Throw with both hands

End 3

- ◉ Stone 5: Free throw (any method)
- ◉ Stone 6: Forward delivery

End 4

- ◉ Stone 7: Backward delivery (face backward and push the stone between the legs)
- ◉ Stone 8: Regular delivery with sweeping

Scoring

At the conclusion of each end, once all 16 stones have been thrown/delivered, students go to the other end of the rink and tally their points.

- ◉ Every stone within the outermost circle is eligible.
- ◉ The stones that are closer to the center of the circle (closer than the opposing team's stones) count 1 point each.
- ◉ The team with the most points in the match wins.

Safety Considerations

To minimize slips and falls, students should have proper footwear. Winter boots or rubber-soled shoes are preferable to street shoes.

Teaching Tips

Team size can be adapted to accommodate more students, but you'll need to reduce the number of throws/deliveries per end or have enough curling stones for each player to complete 2 throws/deliveries. If you divide students into 2 teams of 10 players, for example, you would need 40 curling stones to have 2 throws/deliveries in each end.

DOG SLED RACE

Number of Participants	Grade Level	Activity Level	Playing Area
3 to 5 teams of 3 students	8 and above	High	Snowy area

Recommended Equipment

- 1 toboggan per team
- 8 pylons

Setup

Arrange the pylons in a circle, preferably 20 yards (meters) apart. Mark a start/finish line and divide students into teams. Have teams designate the "dog" (the student pulling the toboggan) and the "mushers" (the students being pulled). Have students assume their positions (on the toboggan or in front of it) and line up the teams at the start/finish line.

How to Play

At the signal to start, the dogs pull their sleds around the circle. The mushers must stay on the toboggan. If they fall off, the team has to start over. The first team to cross the start/finish line with both mushers on the sled wins.

Safety Considerations

If students fall off the toboggan or it overturns, caution other teams to be careful to avoid them when running around the course.

Teaching Tips

If a circle is too easy, set up the pylons to make an obstacle course. For a little more challenge, try the Seeing-Eye Dog Sled Race. For a little less exertion, try Tubers.

Seeing-Eye Dog Sled Race

This race requires 1 more student per team. The dogs wear blindfolds and teammates ("seeing-eye dogs") direct them around the course . Note: seeing-eye dogs are not allowed to touch the blind dogs; they may only direct them verbally.

Tubers

This race involves teams of 2 students: 1 student pushes a teammate on an inner tube around the course.

SNOW TUG-OF-WAR

Number of Participants	Grade Level	Activity Level	Playing Area
2 teams of 4 or more students	8 and above	High	Snowy area

Recommended Equipment

- 1 tug-of-war rope

Setup

Mark a centerline and lay the rope in a straight line, its center (marked with a handkerchief or tape) at the centerline. Divide students into teams and line up each team on either side of the rope.

How to Play

At the signal to start, players pick up the rope and each team pulls. The first team to move the center of the rope 5 yards (meters) past the centerline wins. (You may want to mark these distances before the contest begins.)

Safety Considerations

Be sure to use a traditional tug-of-war rope. Synthetic ropes may burst in the heat of the action.

Teaching Tips

Rather than watch the distance away from the centerline, you could also place colorful cloths or beanbags 5 yards (meters) behind the last student on each end of the rope. The first team to pick up the cloth or beanbag wins.

SNOWBALL FIGHT

Number of Participants	Grade Level	Activity Level	Playing Area
2 teams of 10 to 15 players	8 and above	Medium	Snowy area

Recommended Equipment

- 4 gymnastic mats

Setup

Mark boundary lines in the snow. The playing area should be about the size of a basketball court. Divide the area in half with a centerline.

Divide students into teams and distribute the mats, 2 to a team. Have each team build a prison just inside their own back boundary line.

How to Play

This game is a bit like dodgeball but with a few twists. At the signal to start, players start throwing snowballs at opposing team members, below the waist only. When hit, players must go to the opposing team's prison. To free themselves from prison, prisoners must hit a player from the opposing team. Then the prisoner is set free and the opposing player becomes a prisoner in the opposing team's (also the former prisoner's) prison.

The game lasts only 5 minutes. At the end of the game, the team with the most "free" players (players out of jail) wins.

Rules

- No hitting above the waist. Any player caught aiming above the waist is out of the game.
- If a snowball is caught, the thrower goes to prison.
- If a snowball rebounds off another player and is then caught, both the thrower and the player hit go to prison. The player who catches the snowball stays in the game.

- If a snowball is fumbled (caught but then dropped), the fumbler goes to prison.
- Prisoners may not throw snowballs.
- If the prison gets knocked down, everyone gets out of jail and the prison must be rebuilt. Play does not stop, however. Prison builders can be hit by the opposing team during construction.
- Players may use thrown snowballs or make new ones.

Safety Considerations

To prevent injuries and bruising, do not allow students to pack the snowballs too tightly.

Teaching Tips

This game can be easily moved indoors. Use white foam balls or folded-up socks instead of snowballs.

If students are afraid of getting hit with snowballs, allow them to sit out or have them referee the game.

TOBOGGAN RUN

Number of Participants	Grade Level	Activity Level	Playing Area
5 players per team	13 and above*	Low	Snowy hill

*(college level only)

Recommended Equipment

- None

Setup

Ask for several volunteers to judge the event.

How to Play

Players bring in their own equipment, including building supplies, decorations, materials for the toboggan (anything but steel), and so on. Then, players have a certain amount of time (this should be specified ahead of time—1 to 2 hours is sufficient) to build their toboggans. After construction, toboggans are judged.

To qualify, toboggans must be large enough for 1 driver and solid enough to withstand a race. Up to 5 points are awarded for each of the following criteria:

- Degree of difficulty
- Originality
- Appearance
- Level of detail

After judging, the race begins. Teams line up at the top of a hill and, at the signal to start, race down the hill. The first toboggan to the bottom wins the race, worth 20 points. On the way down, judges are standing by to judge racing criteria (each worth up to 5 points):

- Steering ability
- Quality of ride
- Speed

At the end of the event, the team with the most points wins.

Safety Considerations

To avoid collisions halfway down and at the bottom of the hill, separate teams by at least 2 yards (meters) or have teams go down the hill one at a time (clock their speed with a stopwatch).

Teaching Tips

In addition to the overall championship award, you might consider awarding prizes for certain categories: originality, appearance, and quality of ride, and so on.

This contest is an event in and of itself. Consider making a day of it, offered in conjunction with a chili cook-off and free hot chocolate.

SNOW-BOILING CONTEST

Number of Participants	Grade Level	Activity Level	Playing Area
3 students per team	13 and above*	Low	Outdoor fire pit

*(college level only)

Recommended Equipment

- 1 firewood bundle per team
- 1 kindling bundle per team
- 2 sheets of newspaper per team
- 3 matches per team
- 1 container (pail or other) per team

Setup

Divide students into teams and distribute the firewood, kindling, matches, and newspapers. Give each team a container (a pail, box, or other container) full of snow. Position teams around a large fire pit.

How to Play

At the signal to start, teams race to build a fire and melt the snow in their containers. The first team with boiling water wins.

Safety Considerations

Make sure first-aid supplies are on hand for burns and cuts. Warn students about smoke inhalation and getting too close to the fire, although students should be old enough to know better.

Teaching Tips

If the fire pit is not large enough to accommodate all students, have teams compete individually. Time each team with a stopwatch. The fastest time wins. (To be fair, all ashes should be removed and placed in a metal storage container before a pit can be reused.)

MATCHSTICK PULL

Number of Participants	Grade Level	Activity Level	Playing Area
Any number	8 and above	Low	Anywhere

Recommended Equipment

⊙ 1 wooden match (with head taken off) per team

Setup

Pair up students and have them stand facing each other, their hands folded in a praying position (fingers interlocking) and their index fingers together. Place either end of the match between their index fingers (see illustration). Reprinted, by permission, from the Teaching and Learning Center.

How to Play

At the signal to start, 1 player tries to pull the match away from the opposing player. The player who succeeds is the winner. Play 2 out of 3 (or 3 out of 5, or 5 out of 7, and so on).

Safety Considerations

Make sure the matchsticks are free of slivers before you give them to students.

Teaching Tips

You can organize this as a tournament, having winners play against each other until a class champion emerges.

For more great Inuit games like this one, see *Inuit Games*. This book is available from Kivalliq School Operations, Teaching and Learning Center, BAG 002, Rankin Inlet Nunavut, X0C 0A0. Phone (867) 645-2343.

3-PITCH SNOW BASEBALL

Number of Participants	Grade Level	Activity Level	Playing Area
2 teams of 10 students	6 and above	Medium	Baseball diamond

Recommended Equipment

- 4 bases (colored is best)
- 3 bats (different sizes)
- 1 baseball (colored is best)
- 10 baseball gloves

Setup

Position the bases 15 yards (meters) apart. (It's best to use colored bases and bats so that they are visible in the snow.) Draw a commitment line between third base and home plate, 5 yards (meters) from third base.

Divide students into teams and devise a batting order for each team. Line up the offense behind the backstop, according to batting order, with the last student to bat on the pitching mound. (When it is the pitcher's turn to bat, the team selects another pitcher.) Position the defense: 1 catcher; players on first, second, and third; 1 shortstop between second and third; and 5 outfielders.

How to Play

The game is like 3-Pitch Baseball (see page 139), with three exceptions: (1) it is played in the snow; (2) the base distance is shorter to accommodate winter gear and slower running speed; and (3) sliding into bases is permitted. The team with the most runs at the end of the game wins.

Safety Considerations

If one is available, use a safety base on first. This base is twice as wide as regular bases, which will enable the first-base player to keep a foot on the bag without tripping runners—especially when playing in winter boots. To prevent head and face injuries, require catchers and pitchers to wear face masks.

Teaching Tips

To accommodate a range of batting skills among students, have bats of different sizes and weights available. (Beginners do better with lighter bats.) Encourage students to wear oversized baseball gloves so that they can wear warm gloves underneath.

To be fair, make sure both teams get equal times at bat. Either limit the game to 5 innings or, 10 minutes before the end of class, call out "Ten minutes!" to let students know that the starting defense will get a last turn at bat.

part III

Adding Your Own Games

chapter 16

Your Games

N ow that the games, contests, relays, challenges, and activities in this book have whetted your appetite for fun, don't stop now. Create some of your own!

The games and variations throughout this book may help spur some ideas. For example, Scooter Noodle Hockey (see page 188) is simply hockey using different equipment. Boor's Ultimate Medical Dodgeball (see page 60) is like regular dodgeball but with different (and more complex) rules. Use similar modifications and come up with your own special rules for any of the games presented in this book, or create your own games from scratch. Involve your students, too. Challenge them to think up some exciting variations to the games presented in this book or have them create new games of their own.

Another effective way to stimulate the brainstorming process is to use the Game Generator.

GAME GENERATOR

Put simply, the Game Generator is the starting ground for devising a game. It assumes certain criteria have been set. The six modules on the Game Generator represent these criteria, including (1) the number of participants, (2) the competitiveness, (3) the equipment used, (4) the skill involved, (5) how players will move, and (6) the level of energy required. Knowing all criteria

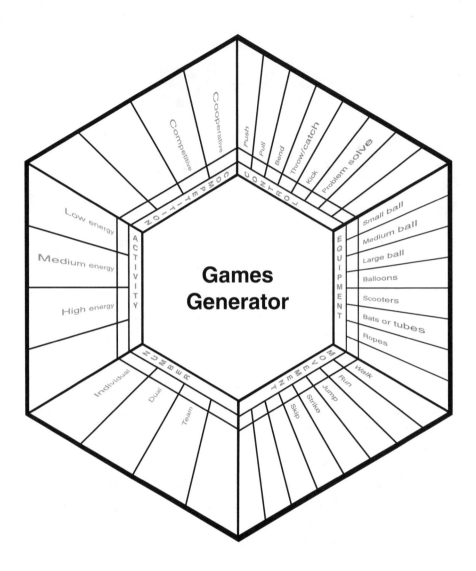

ahead of time is not necessary, but you have to start with something.

This section explains the use of the Game Generator step by step. In keeping with the spirit of fun and games in this book, however, we suggest that you make it a game in and of itself. Divide students into teams of 4 to 5. Photocopy the Game Generator and the Game Recorder (page 268) . Check off at least one component in each Game Generator module and then distribute the copies to each team. Students use the checked components as the major features of their game. At the end of class, students vote on the best game.

You may want to check off different components on each sheet to discourage the temptation to copy or steal others' ideas. Starting students out with different components can also help in effectively using available resources. For example, if your school does not have scooters available, it's probably not a good idea to allow students to come up with games that require scooters. Likewise, if the school gymnasium is too small for group and team games, it's best to have students come up with individual or dual games (see the Number module). *Note:* Additional and unusual components should be listed on the blank lines of each module.

Before going into the specifics of the six Game Generator modules, let's consider an example. Suppose you ask students to develop a low-energy, competitive game that is a team event, uses ropes, and involves jumping, throwing, and catching.

The game might go something like this: 2 players from a team twirl a jump rope. The rest of the team lines up to jump, off to the side of the twirling rope and just behind the middle of the rope. One by one, jumpers move under the rope, jump over it without hitting or interfering with the rope in any way, turn and catch a ball, throw the ball to a teammate, and exit the jumping area. In other words, Jumper 1 moves to the jumping area, jumps, and then turns around to catch a ball thrown by Jumper 2, who is standing in line. Then Jumper 2 moves under the rope while Jumper 1 throws the ball to Jumper 3 (standing in line) and exits the jumping area. Jumper 2 turns around, catches the ball. Jumper 3 moves under the rope while Jumper 2 throws the ball to Jumper 4, and so on. The object of the game is to see how many people on a team can successfully jump without stopping the rope. The team with the most consecutive jumpers wins.

On the Game Generator, the game would look like this.

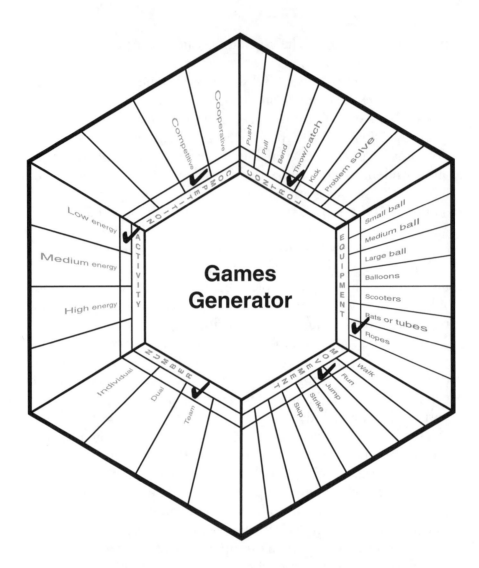

While the explanation communicates the main thrust of this game, it could be presented more clearly. The Game Recorder (page 268) helps to do just that. Before explaining the Game Recorder and illustrating how this rope jumping/throwing/catching game would be recorded, however, let's go through each module of the Game Generator, step by step.

Step 1: Determine the number of students involved.

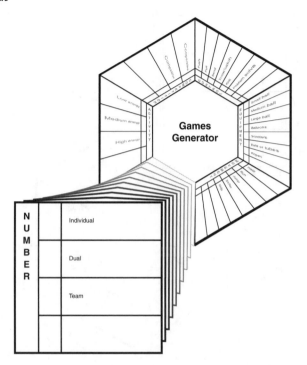

The Number module defines the number of students involved in the game. Individual activities involve 1 student. Chapter 7, Individual Challenges, includes many games of this kind. Dual activities involve pairs of students, each one challenging the other. Thumb Wrestling (page 112) and Kangaroo Hop (page 106) are examples of dual activities. Team events typically involve 2 or more teams of 2 or more players competing as a team. Games such as 3-Pitch Baseball (page 139) and Tubers (page 246) are examples of team games.

Step 2. Decide how competitive you want the game to be.

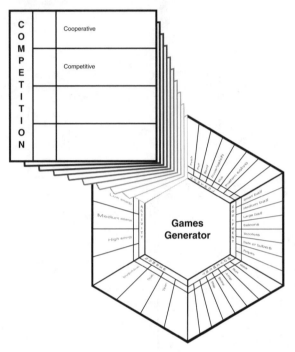

Players can compete against one another or work together as a team to overcome common obstacles. Relays, races, tugs-of-war, sport games, contests, and the challenges in chapter 7 are competitive, although team cooperation is certainly involved in many cases. Games such as Sinking Island (page 13), Crotchety Pipe Walk (page 45) , and Going Nuts (page 53) require cooperation.

Step 3. Identify the equipment to be used.

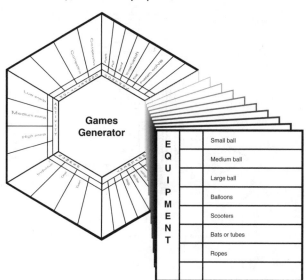

Obviously, equipment must be available to use in a game. In most schools, equipment such as basketballs and volleyballs—as well as jerseys (or pinnys) to distinguish teams and pylons to define goals and obstacles—are readily available. Hockey sticks, noodles, and curling equipment may not be, however. Pay attention to the equipment needs of each game. If you create a game that requires equipment you don't have, no one will be able to play. Of course, there's always the option of creating a game that requires no equipment. Games such as Team Backside Tug-of-War (page 103) and Stork Stand (page 108) are examples of no-equipment games. Note: It may be helpful to note the number of equipment pieces available. Use the space to the right of each piece of equipment.

Think about safety as well. For example, gymnastic mats can make a game safer, as will using noodles instead of bats or sticks. Some important safety issues are identified in chapter 1. There is also a separate section on the Game Recorder to address safety concerns.

Step 4. Identify the skill involved.

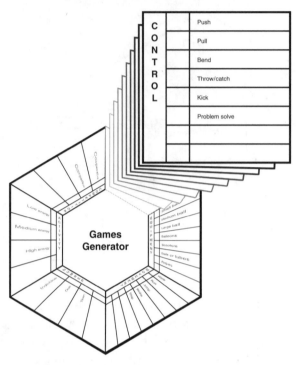

The Skill module deals with the skill required to play the game, namely, how equipment is controlled, the physical movement required, and mental skill. This module presents an opportunity to target certain skills in need of development. Therefore, some thought should go into planning this module. For example, the movement of kicking increases muscle tone and improves flexibility and balance. The real challenge lies in creating a fun game that involves these skills. Kicking games don't have to be kicking contests. The game should be fun. Soccer Volleyball (page 226) and Team Hackey Sac Dribble (page 125) are two examples.

Don't forget the mental aspects of game playing, either. Games of strategy require mental thought and preparation, not to mention brainstorming and team cooperation. Some games that involve mental skill as well as physical movement are Hoop Escape (page 66) and Boor's Ultimate Medical Dodgeball (page 60).

Step 5. Identify the movement involved.

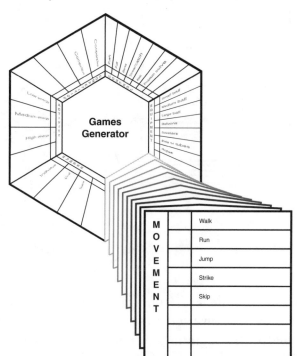

The Movement module, at first glance, seems redundant to the Skill module. However, each game requires different player movements. Traditional games like soccer or basketball require running and jumping, but if scooter boards are used, "rolling" is required. Standing games could involve coin games or contests such as Squash Serve or Fowl Shooting.

Step 6. Determine the energy level of the game.

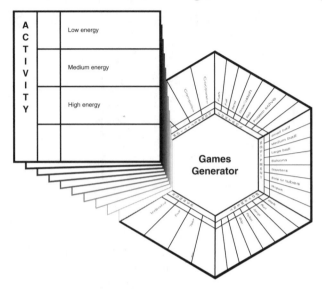

The Activity module is an important one. For starters, you want to be in control of how riled up students get in class. When devising a game for the beginning or end of class, a low-energy game such as Blind Puzzle (page 6) would enable students to warm up or warm down gradually. Likewise, if the class will consist of several high-energy games in a row, breaking them up with a medium-energy game such as Wheeling Around (page 56) may help students recover.

Many of the games in this book have been developed with the Game Generator. Take ABS Rollerball (page 63), for example. I wanted a game that involved many students, was cooperative, used unusual equipment (like ABS pipe), required more thinking than physical movement, and used little energy. As I thought about increasing the challenge, a number of interesting variations emerged. For example, Coiled Rollerball (page 64), Uphill Rollerball (page 64), and No-Hands Rollerball (page 64).

GAME RECORDER

Once the game has been devised, it's time to translate that information to a usable game format. As described earlier, an endless stream of plays and instructions can get confusing. The easiest method for recording games—at least, the easiest I've come up with—is using the Game Recorder.

If involving students in the game-generating process, you'll need to provide each team with several copies of the Game Recorder. Once students have written their game on paper, they may need to revise it. Then teams can take turns teaching their games to the class. At that point, classmates may have some revisions or suggestions to make the game more challenging, interesting, or fun. These ideas should be recorded, either by the team presenting a game or by you. Then, at last, the final game should be recorded on the Game Recorder.

Designed to include all important aspects of a game, the Game Recorder includes the following main sections:

- Title
- Number of Participants
- Grade Level
- Recommended Equipment
- Activity Level
- Playing Area
- Setup
- How to Play
- Safety Considerations
- Teaching Tips

Specific Game Generator modules apply to each section. (Many modules are involved in several sections.) A detailed description of each section follows.

Title

Identify the game with a title. It is a lot quicker, and clearer, to say "Let's play Quicksand" than it is to say "Let's play that game with the tarp and the Xs where everyone has to walk across the grid, which is written on paper and not the tarp, trying again and again if they step off the trail."

To increase efficiency of communication, title each new game specifically. With a little creativity, game titles can get students

GAME RECORDER

Title _____

Number of Participants _____

Grade Level _____

Recommended Equipment_____

_____

_____

Activity Level_____

Playing Area_____

Setup _____

_____

_____

_____

How to Play _____

_____

_____

_____

Rules_____

_____

Safety Considerations _____

_____

Teaching Tips _____

_____

Variations _____

_____

into the spirit of the game before the game has even begun. The title of Quicksand sounds more fun than Crossing the Grid.

Number of Participants

This section of the Game Recorder seems self-explanatory, but it's not. Although the Number module on the Game Generator frames this section, it needs further clarification. For example, available equipment will determine how many students can play at one time. The Movement module of the Game Generator also comes into play. If the game involves running, it may be best to group the players in teams. Other considerations in this section include what works best for the age group and available space.

After considering these factors, complete this section of the Game Recorder by answering the following questions.

- How many students can play?
- Are teams involved?
- How many per team?

Grade Level

Grade level is the product of several Game Generator modules: Activity, Skill, Movement, Equipment, and Competition. A rather complicated judgment based on an understanding of children, safety factors, and many of the game's components, determining the appropriate grade level is best left to the final stages of completing the Game Recorder. Once the game is defined, explained, and understandable to all, think through the safety concerns and visualize actual play. Then use your discretion.

As you've likely noticed, the games in this book do not have a cut-off age. This is because adults tend to enjoy children's games as much as, if not more than, kids do. *Note:* Modifying the equipment slightly can often make the game more suitable for younger children, for example, using balloons or foam balls instead of traditional sport balls.

If involving students in the game-generating process, it's best if you determine the appropriate grade level. Younger students, in particular, should not be responsible for completing this section. Suggest the appropriate grade level of the game and then solicit students' suggestions, reminding them to consider the skill necessary to play the game well and safely.

Recommended Equipment

This section of the Game Recorder is straightforward. Transfer the equipment directly from the Equipment module. Then consider a few other factors. If the game involves teams, do jerseys (or pinnys) need to be used to distinguish players? If the game involves obstacles, goals, boundaries, start/finish lines, and so on, will pylons be needed? Also consider safety when completing this section. Include equipment that will (1) ensure the safety of participants (for example, gymnastic mats to pad the playing surface or walls) or (2) help make the game safer and more enjoyable for all (for example, use of noodles instead of bats or sticks).

Activity Level

This section is another straightforward transfer, from the Game Generator Activity module. (If students are creating the games, the Activity module should have been identified ahead of time.) This section will have an impact on later sections of the Game Recorder, namely, How to Play, Rules, Safety Considerations. In general, the more active the game, the greater the number of rules and safety considerations.

Playing Area

Playing Area is the result of several Game Generator modules: Number, Equipment, Movement, and Activity. Specifics are important here. For example, it may be tempting to identify a gymnasium as the ideal playing area when all you really need is a large enclosed space with a flat floor. In this case, the game could likely be played in a long hallway.

Describe the playing area specifically, then identify other places the game could be played successfully and safely. This will help you identify alternate games, for use in the Variations section of the Game Recorder.

Setup

This section involves the Number, Equipment, and Skill modules of the Game Generator. As you visualize actual play, notice the playing area. Are boundaries or start/finish lines involved? Does equipment need to be positioned ahead of time? Now visualize the start of the game. If teams are involved, how should they be determined? Where should they be situated? Which team will start the game? If the game involves detailed rules, such as the list of items to find in Scavenger Hunt (page 14), will students need a photocopy? Finally, are there safety considerations? For example, does anything need to be removed from the playing area?

Every game—even a simple relay race—requires some sort of setup. Make sure the Setup section explains everything necessary to get the game started.

How to Play

This is the meat-and-potatoes section, including every aspect of the game—and, thus, all six Game Generator modules. It's easiest to approach step by step.

1. If the game can be compared to a traditional game, or even a game in this book, start there. Then summarize any differences in play or rules. This gives participants a quick sense of the game.

2. Describe the progression of play. At least summarize the game in the beginning of this section. Then you can go into specifics.

3. Think about the rules. If they can be explained in the progression of the game, do it that way. If the game involves numerous rules, however, grouping them separately is probably a good idea. If necessary, use subcategories to organize the rules. For example, in Curling Funspiel (page 243), Delivery and Throwing is separate from Scoring. For a sport game, the rules could be grouped by offensive and defensive infractions. They can also be lumped together but should be listed clearly and logically. In Recreational Soccer

(page 193), for example, offenses are italicized for easy reference.

4. Last but certainly not least, who wins the game?

Note: If helpful in learning the game, strategies can also be included in this section. But if strategy formulation is part of the fun, it may be best to let students figure out playing tactics for themselves.

Safety Considerations

Safety is always a concern when creating, teaching, and playing games. Thus, it should considered for every module of the Game Generator. For example, is any of the equipment potentially hazardous? What about the playing area? Could mats and other padding ensure safety without interfering with play? If the game is active (a high-energy game), what are the risks of students engaging in rough play or running into something? Are many students involved at one time and, if so, could they trip over or collide with one another? How competitive is the game? Could students become frustrated and aggressive? What skills are involved? Might students tear a muscle or sprain a joint? Should students warm up/down before and after the game? How might players' movements create a safety hazard for each other?

General safety concerns were addressed in Organizing the Fun at the beginning of this book, but a few cautions are worth repeating here.

- Check the playing area for potholes, broken glass, stones, puddles, and so on before you set up.
- Never designate a wall as a start/finish or boundary.
- Pad stationary equipment, such as volleyball or badminton net poles, in case students run into them during play.
- If the game involves contact with a ball, as it does in the myriad games in this book, consider using soft balls such as foam balls and bladders.
- Post an emergency plan and enforce it. (You may want to hold practice drills every month for younger students.)

◎ Make sure that someone qualified in CPR and first aid is readily available for emergencies.

◎ Require proper safety attire: eye protection, helmets with face masks, shin pads, and so on.

◎ Discourage rough play. If some students are roughhousing or engaging in other shenanigans, stop play immediately. If those same students continue playing roughly, eject them from the game.

◎ Give students an "out" if they need it.

◎ If you or a student spots a potential hazard, stop the game to remove the hazard or change the game to minimize risk of injury.

Teaching Tips

The final section of the Game Recorder is used as a catchall. List other considerations that don't fit into the earlier sections. For example, suggest different setups that will modify the game slightly, or list some of the strategies of the game that teachers or coaches should be aware of but that students should figure out while playing the game.

Include variations in this section as well. As I discovered in devising ABS Rollerball (page 63), variations are endless. (If involved in the game-generating process, students will likely have lots of ideas for modifying new games.) Perhaps a different rule or piece of equipment would make the game more interesting, challenging, or fun. For example, Four-Goal Soccer (page 204) becomes a much more entertaining game when played with a bladder ball.

PUTTING IT ALL TOGETHER

Now we return to our example of the jump rope game developed earlier. This game would be translated to the Game Recorder as follows.

GAME RECORDER

Title _Catch Jump Rope_

Number of Participants _4 or more players per team_

Grade Level _2 and above_

Recommended Equipment _> 1 jump rope per team_

> 1 ball per team

Activity Level _Low_

Playing Area _Anywhere_

Setup _Divide students into teams and group them around the playing area. Have each team designate 2 rope twirlers (the rest of the students will jump). Distribute the ropes and balls. Position the rope twirlers on either end of the rope and have them start circling the rope. Jumpers should be lined up in single file on one side of the rope, just behind the middle of the rope, and the second jumper in line should be holding the ball._

How to Play _At the signal to start, the first jumper on each team moves in to the jumping area, jumps, and then turns around to catch a ball thrown by jumper 2, who is the next jumper in line. Then Jumper 2 moves under the rope while Jumper 1 throws the ball to Jumper 3 (standing in line) and exits the jumping area. Jumper 2 jumps, then turns around and catches the ball (thrown by Jumper 3). Jumper 3 moves under the rope while jumper 2 throws the ball to Jumper 4 and exits the jumping area, and so on._

The object of the game is to see how many people on a team can successfully jump without stopping the rope. Teammates call out the

number of jumps as jumpers complete their turns. The team with the
most consecutive jumpers wins.

Rules _If jumpers hit or interfere with the rope in any way, the count_
starts again.

Safety Considerations _Make sure students do not trip on the rope._
For younger and inexperienced students, it may be a good idea to pad
the surface. (Playing on a carpeted area would work as well.) To reduce
the risk of shin splints, do not play this game longer than 30 minutes.

Teaching Tips _If everyone wants to jump, work twirler substitutions_
into the game. For example, the first student to jump could take over
for one twirler and the second student could take over for the other
twirler.

Variations _This game can be easily adapted to a race. Rather than_
count jumps, teams race to complete the cycle: all team members
must move in, jump, catch the ball, and move out. If one teammate hits
or stops the rope, all teammates must start over. The first team to
complete the cycle wins.

A FINAL WORD

When all is said and done, you and your students will have cre-
ated games that can be enjoyed for many years to come. If you
come up with some really great games, please fax them to John
Byl, Redeemer University College, (905) 648-2134. If I receive
enough new game ideas, they may just end up in a new games
book! (All contributors will be credited for their ideas, of course.)

About the Author

J ohn Byl, PhD, is a professor of physical education and the intramural director at Redeemer University College in Hamilton, Ontario, Canada. He directed physical education programs and coached various sports for 23 years at the community, high school, and college levels. He is a national board member of the Canadian Intramural Recreation Association, an executive member of the Ontario College Committee on Campus Recreation, and a vice president of the Canadian Intramural Recreation Association—Ontario.

Byl received his PhD in organization, administration and policy, specializing in the social foundations division, from the State University of New York at Buffalo. He earned a masters of human kinetics degree from the University of Windsor and a bachelor of physical education degree from the University of British Columbia

Author of *Organizing Successful Tournaments* and *Minor Games Manual*, Byl has also contributed chapters to several other books and has published many articles and proceedings on sports and physical education.

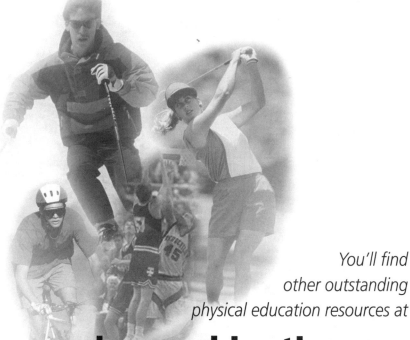